No Strings Attached

A GUIDE TO
A BETTER RELATIONSHIP
WITH YOUR
GROWN-UP CHILD

by Howard M. Halpern, Ph.D.

Simon and Schuster New York

Published by Simon and Schuster
A Division of Gulf & Western Corporation
Simon & Schuster Building
Rockefeller Center
1230 Avenue of the Americas
New York, New York 10020

Designed by Jill Weber
Manufactured in the United States of America
1 2 3 4 5 6 7 8 9 10

Library of Congress Cataloging in Publication Data

Halpern, Howard Marvin, date.
No strings attached.

Includes bibliographical references.
1. Parent and child. 2. Conflict of
generations. 3. Interpersonal relations.
I. Title. II. Title: Grown-up child.
HQ755.85.H34 301.42'7 79-18605
ISBN 0-671-24047-1

Acknowledgments

I wish to thank the many fathers and mothers, often strangers, who permitted me to interview them and who responded with such candidness about their relationships with their grown-up sons and daughters. I also want to thank my patients who, for over a quarter of a century, have shared so much with me about the parent-child bond at all ages.

I am grateful also to those whose help, by adding a little here and a little there, sprinkled spice throughout this book: Lorraine Rosenthal, David Doroff, Jim Ranck, John Kildahl and especially Jane Goldman who penciled through the finished manuscript, making suggestions that helped clarify many points.

And a hug to my daughters, Shari and Dina, who contributed as research assistants and by their patience with the many "lost weekends" when I was holed up writing. As they become more grown-up and independent, they challenge me to ask myself what our relationship is all about when they need me for less.

A special warm thank you to Lori Jacobs, who typed, corrected, criticized and commented on this manuscript, chapter by chapter, with acute, astute and caring judgment.

Deep appreciation also goes to Ellen Levine and to Peter Schwed, who were nurturant and encouraging throughout.

HOWARD HALPERN
New York, March 1979

To my father, Samuel Halpern
and my mother, Dora Halpern,
who raised six of us to adulthood.

Though you have been dead for many years,
I increasingly marvel
at your continued existence in me,
sometimes to my frustration and chagrin
and often to my pleasure.

Contents

Chapter 11 GOING MY WAY 214
Your child's becoming a self-sufficient adult offers you, the parent, a chance for a new life. How to make and enjoy your own Declaration of Independence.

"Small children were like planets, harnessed to their parents in orderly orbits by the firmly balanced forces of attraction and resistance. But these orbits as children age became more comet-like; your offspring began swinging in wild ellipses in and out of your own force field—almost breaking away entirely, but then swooping back in to set off a riot of sparks and static with their conflicting charges. One didn't issue instructions to comets. Grown children did what they had to do, and parents could only grit their teeth and watch and pray for them to get through it."

—Lisa Alther, *Kinflicks*

Prelude

The pain and bewilderment were apparent as she spoke of her son. "He complained I called him too much, and he began to hang up as soon as he heard my voice. I tried to explain how important it was to me to keep in touch, but the very next day he got an unlisted number. I couldn't believe it. I feel completely cut off from him. Is there anything wrong with a mother's wanting to speak to her son once in a while?"

Another mother talked of her frustrations in dealing with her married daughter: "I start off each visit determined we'll get along well, but soon we're into an angry, awful scene. I don't even know how it happens, but it leaves me feeling dreadful."

A father complained, "You psychologists are always saying everything's the parents' fault. Well, I've worked hard all my life, and here's my son, twenty-six years old, who's had a dozen different jobs and doesn't stick to one of them. Twenty-six and he's nowhere. How's that my fault? I still have to give him some money, and at times he moves back home for a while because he's so broke. I'm sick of it and worried about what will happen after we're gone."

I have now heard so many similar bitter and disillusioned laments that it's become very evident to me that there is a widespread malaise among the parents of many grown-up offspring. As a parent, you know how much of your life, for so many years, had centered in your children. You couldn't begin to tally the hours, the dollars, the caring and the worry. And the chances are you had taken it for granted that by now, with their adulthood, you would be able to reap the rewards of a harmonious and gratifying relationship, free from the demands of their younger years and the conflicts of their adolescence. But instead you find that with one of your children—maybe with more—the interaction is so tense, so soured with disappointment or anger, or so chilled with distance and frost that you despair over what has happened to this relationship in which you have invested so much love and around which you had spun so many dreams.

Even where the situation was not grim, where the relationship was mostly satisfying, parents approached me with many perplexing questions, as if issues had arisen that they had no experiences to draw from in their past that could help them.

> I know my son is living with his girl friend at college. Now he's bringing her home for Thanksgiving and he expects they'll share his room, but I'm terribly uncomfortable about it. I'm afraid if I don't permit it, he won't stay with us at all.
>
> My son and his family are thinking of moving 3,000 miles away. It would be awful for me not to see them and, in particular, my grandchildren. And my grandchildren are very attached to us. I'd like to ask my son not to do it, but I know it's not my business. Or is it?
>
> Should I let my seventeen-year-old daughter stay out all night on the weekends the way she wants to?
>
> My daughter and son-in-law want to borrow money from us as a down payment on a home and have asked that it be interest-free. We can afford it, though we're not exactly rich, but I'm not sure it's fair to us or to them.

> I am widowed and not able to get around as well as I used to when I was younger. My children don't live that far away, and it would be so helpful if they would just come over every week or so and say, "Can I help you with something?" Or just visit. But they are always too busy. I know they have families of their own and lots to do, but am I really asking too much?

These can be very knotty questions and have complexities and subtleties that we will look at later. But what gives them the *emotional power* I can hear in the troubled voices of these parents is the fear that if they do not handle these issues right, they can badly damage their relationship with their children. And that, as you well know, is a very worrisome thing.

Are You Obsolete?

No longer do you have the control of your children's lives that you had when they were younger and bound to you by their needs and by your set of rules and expectations. There was a time when your life and theirs were daily intertwined. You set the tone and pace of the household and of their lives. From table manners to sexuality, from where they would live to how they would spend their summers, from whom they could bring home as friends to how they were to behave with adults, from duties and responsibilities to taboos and restrictions, you set the guidelines, and their dependence on you usually induced them to adhere to your injunctions. Because for them, your arms, your home and your ways delineated the known world. You were the center of their universe, and to a great extent they were the center of yours. But as they grew, their known world got wider, and they ventured forth and discovered new lands, new ways, and new strengths. They entered territory familiar to them but a dark continent to you, a region of relationships and choices that was theirs alone, and from which you were excluded. What a blow to your old sense of knowing all, of making decisions for them based on your own more seasoned perspectives and your power!

What is your appropriate role in your children's lives if you don't have the old functions of control and protection and nurturance? As parent–caretakers, you are mostly obsolete. Like someone replaced by a machine or computer, your old function no longer exists. Yet you are not quit of your involvement. And unlike someone whose job has been phased out and who is either fired or given a new title with a new job description, you still carry the title "parent." This appellation indicates that you brought certain young people you call your children—into the world, but it tells you nothing about what you are to them now or who they are to you. Yet "parent" you remain. In *A Month of Sundays,* John Updike writes: "Society in its conventional wisdom sets a term to childhood; of parenthood there is no riddance. Though the child be a sleek senator of seventy, and the parent a twisted hulk in a wheelchair, the wreck must still grapple with the ponderous sceptre of parenthood."*

So you've got this lifetime appointment. Wonderingly you grasp the ponderous but powerless sceptre. But in the everyday world, *what is the parent of an adult child for*? Even the word "child" confuses the issue. When does it mean "offspring" and when does it mean "little and young"? And how often does this double meaning taint our view of our grown-up sons and daughters? I have often approached parents of children in their twenties, thirties or even older, saying I'd like to interview them about some of the problems of being the parent of an adult and to my surprise (at least at first) found that they would look startled and say, "Do you mean me? I don't have adult children." Their image of their offspring lagged far behind the chronological actuality. For example, I interviewed a couple where the wife, who had been one of the "startled" parents explained, "We may not choose to think of them as adults, but they are and we must accept the fact. . . . They are twenty-five, twenty-three and twenty-one. I don't feel old enough to have children that age. Yet they are adults because they are leading their own lives and doing their own thing. I may not like what they do, but they're doing it and they're not asking me. . . . But for me just the idea that chronologically they are that old! The first time you asked me

* John Updike, *A Month of Sundays* (New York: Knopf, 1975), p. 118.

what it's like to be the parent of an adult I had to stop and think what that meant, because I thought of myself as the parent of grown-up *children* but never thought of them as adults." Her husband added, "There's an old saying, 'The older they get, the bigger they get; the bigger they get, the bigger the problems; and the greater the problems, the more you think of them as *children*.' "

Once you have acknowledged that your children are indeed adults, we can begin our efforts to define the relationship of parent to adult child by agreeing that what you have with your children is a special and unique human bond, beginning with the incomparable miracle of birth, then marked by your dedication to keeping these helpless creatures alive and healthy, and later by your daily participation in the stresses and wonder of their growth and unfolding. Whether your current concerns well up from the pain of a deep rift and bitter disillusionment, or some vague uneasiness and disappointment, or simply from anxiety that you might mishandle the new conflicts that come with your son's or daughter's adulthood, you may well have need to take a fresh look at your relationship with your son or daughter. You may need to tilt the prism through which you have always perceived them and find a new perspective, a new coloration.

Both Sides Now

The father who called saying "You psychologists are always saying everything's the parents' fault" is voicing a commonly held complaint, one with much truth to it. As psychologists and psychoanalysts began to comprehend the impact of parents on the development of the child's personality and problems, some of them did get into parent-blaming. And even those who did not seemed at times to be criticizing parents merely by setting forth their findings about parental influence. Thus, they often gave "scientific" backing to the accusations of their children.

In *Fear of Flying,* Erica Jong noted the powerful tie between parent and child that is reflected in these denunciations: "Parents and children are umbilically attached and not only in the womb. Mysterious forces bind them. If my generation is going to spend its time denouncing our parents, then maybe we should allow our parents equal time."* We parents often have had a "bum rap," and when I have felt unfairly indicted, I have often wanted equal time, not only to defend myself but to indict back. But I know that if we emphasize child-blaming, it would be as counterproductive as has been the period of parent-blaming. It would continue the myth that there is a culprit to be found, that one party is "good" and the other is "bad." It would not only heat up the conflict but would be a false approach. The truth is that there has been a very long and complex interaction between you and your child in which all involved have contributed to bring about whatever trouble you may be having. If you want to bring more harmony into that relationship and into your life, your best bet is to try to understand that complexity, because even though it is a complicated matter, understanding it is a necessary prelude to changing it. And most often it can be changed. In working with parents who are unhappy about their relationship with their children, I have found two things I can tell you with certainty:

There are reasons why it went wrong.
There are things you can do to make it better.

* Erica Jong, *Fear of Flying* (New York: Holt, Rinehart and Winston, 1973), p. 43.

CHAPTER 1

There Goes That Song Again

When you and your grown-up child clash, each of you will believe, with all sincerity, that you are right. I've listened to a mother complain, "If Mark would be in touch with me more often on his own, I wouldn't have to call him and keep after him about it." And I've heard Mark say, "If she didn't make me feel so guilty each time I called about not calling her sooner, our conversations would be more pleasant, and I'd probably feel like calling more often." I've had a father tell me, "Susan is making a big mess of her life, but she won't take any advice from me," and later I listened to Susan complain, "If he didn't always make me feel like I'm incapable of handling my own life, there's lots of things I'd like to discuss with him."

Who is right? Obviously both, if you look at it from inside of each person's perspective and feelings. And each is frustrated and saddened by the conflict and distance. For the adult offspring, there is often a feeling of the parent as enemy—as someone who threatens to intrude or engulf, or demand and command, or accuse and criticize.

And for you as the parent, there may be profound disappointment, the pain of a dream shattered, the sadness of a loss of closeness, the hurt and bewilderment of being shut out, and the haunting doubt that perhaps you failed in this supremely important role in your life. Some of you find that your children are ungiving strangers, cool and unreachable, perhaps living a life foreign to what you had envisioned for them—even alien to anything you can feel comfortable about. Others may find that your children are not merely distant, but chronically hostile and easily angered by remarks or actions that, as far as you are concerned, were nothing but well intentioned. Still others may have the opposite grievance, worrying that your child has not matured sufficiently, has not become independent and self-sufficient, is still leaning on you emotionally, and perhaps financially, long after he should be on his own feet.

What has gone wrong here? And what can you do about it now?

As I have already indicated, something can be done to improve your relationship with your grown-up children. But it is not going to be easy because you will be up against formidable obstacles that exist both outside and within yourself. One obstacle is that your actions and theirs are often governed, not by rational and considered judgment, but by emotions and needs that originate deep inside you and stem from your own personal history as a young child. At times our behavior seems controlled by emotions that are clearly self-defeating if not downright off the wall when we look at them later from a more sober perspective. Sometimes we can hardly believe we did this or said that. It is as if something had come over us, as if some powerful emotional state had risen up from inside.

And indeed it has, because we know that in every human being there is an *inner child,* a part of us that is an emotional hangover from our childhood.* Inscribed in the brain cells of each one of

* This "inner child" is similar to the idea of the Child ego state developed by Eric Berne, *Transactional Analysis in Psychotherapy* (New York: Grove, 1961), although I include much of what he would call the Parent ego state. It is probably even more closely related to the construct of W. Hugh Missildine as developed in *Your Inner Child of the Past* (New York: Simon & Schuster, 1963). He wrote, "Whether we like it or not, we are simultaneously the child we once were, who lives in the emotional atmosphere of the past and often interferes in the present, and an adult who tries to forget the past and live wholly in the present." (p. 14)

us are the "videotapes" of every childhood experience and all the feelings that went with them, including fear, love, anger, joy, dependency, self-centeredness, neediness, insecurity, inadequacy, etc. Various kinds of scientific and clinical data have given us evidence of this. One neurosurgeon found that when he stimulated certain very tiny areas of the cerebral cortex with an electrode, memories of past events were relived in full detail, as if they were being played back as a videotape, complete with the words, sounds and, most important, the *emotions* that were felt at the time of the original event.* Similar recall has been attained many times through hypnosis. It would seem that everything that ever happened to us, including those countless moments we thought were forgotten, has been recorded and stored.

Also registered in our neurons during our childhood are our parents' commands, prejudices, injunctions and rules for living (just as our parents' brain cells contain the voices of their own parents, and our children's brain cells contain our voices). The combination of those tapes of all our early childhood feelings and reactions and the tapes of all the ways our parents behaved and all the injunctions and prescriptions for living they gave us compose an emotional memory bank to which I will refer as our *inner child.* These stored transcriptions from our childhood can later be "switched on," not by electrodes, but by an experience, thought or interaction. Once this inner child is switched on, it is replayed in the present as current feelings and behavior without our awareness that this is taking place, and therefore without being modified by our more mature experience, knowledge and accumulated wisdom. This happens to every one of us, and it is important for you to recognize that you, as well as your offspring, can be unwittingly influenced and ruled by the feelings and perspectives of your childhood.

One of the most profound feelings inscribed in our inner child, from our own infancy and early childhood, is the fear of being unloved and abandoned. We've all known this feeling, even if our parents were most loving and attentive. There were still times when their attention had to go elsewhere. They had to leave us for a few minutes or hours or days, or they put us in our cribs and left the room, or they were deeply preoccupied and inatten-

* Wilder Penfield, "Memory Mechanisms," *AMA Archives of Neurology and Psychiatry* (67/1952): 178–98.

tive, or whatever. Our emotional reaction to these events was sometimes catastrophic. After all, our very lives and well-being depended on our parent(s) being there for us when we were helpless infants and small children. And our sense of time was very different from what it became later. For the young child, this one moment is the only moment. Now is all and forever. If mommy and daddy are gone *now,* they are gone for all eternity. You've probably seen the arrival of a baby-sitter trigger this kind of traumatic reaction in your small child when he realized it meant you were going out. Will you ever return? And out of reach of your conscious efforts to retrieve it but stored in your inner child are, most assuredly, similar catastrophic emotional memories.

For our inner child, whose greatest fear is abandonment, it can sometimes become crucial to keep our own children closely tied to us, to share their lives with them, *as if they are the comforting parents and we are the terrified child, afraid we will lose them forever if they stray too far.* That insecure child within us can't really believe our offspring can grow in their own directions, can become quite separate from us, and yet can still love us. Like the child who panics when he loses his parents in a department store, we can't believe that they'll care enough to seek us out and want to be with us. So our inner child slips into old ways of trying to hold on to our offspring and not permit them to stray.

In fiction, one of the most honest observations of a parent's wish to hold on to her offspring and not let them stray is found in *Kinflicks,* where Ginny's mother, Mrs. Babcock, is looking back at her rearing of her three children, now grown.

> If *she* could have run things, she'd have arrested their development at around age five. She had adored their compact little bodies at that age. . . . When they'd dance to their records, they were so breathtakingly graceful and unselfconscious that tears would come to her eyes. And yet they had still required her in other ways, had scrambled onto her lap for cuddling and tickling and reassurance.
>
> But there was a descent into a pit before them. They grew up overnight upon starting school and insisted on doing everything for themselves and no longer sought the safety of her lap for recharging. Having finally learned to accept responsibility for them gracefully, she was now sud-

> denly expected to unlearn all that and let go of them. And then the physical transformations—the boys' voices began cracking, they became awkward and as timid as two year olds, but covered it over with an irritating braggadocio. Ginny had begun menstruating, had developed hips and breasts. . . . And out of it all would come children of their own, to whom *they* would look wistfully, hoping for more original things.*

And Ginny is clearly aware of that part of her mother that wants to hold her offspring forever to her as little needful children. But despite her insight and her awareness of the grief her mother has experienced as the children drifted away, when Ginny is later talking about her own daughter, she complains, "Wendy stubbornly insisted on a cup when I offered my breast. I was destroyed. I had intended to nurse her for at *least* another year, in keeping with my Earth Mother self-image. This was my first hint of the enormity of my folly: Wendy was supposed to be an extension of me, my lifeline to the Future. Was it really possible that she might have things *she* wanted to do?"†

At least in part, Ginny's mother's need to "arrest their development at age five" and Ginny's dismay at Wendy's rejection of her breast come from some deep inner child part of them that prizes attachment and holding on as a way of feeling secure and avoiding aloneness. Certainly parents are not all "inner child" in relation to their children. Hopefully, the major part of us, the part that is primarily directing our feelings and actions in that relationship, is the mature parenting part of us. And that mature parenting part has as its aim the wish to help the offspring become separate, self-reliant individuals. After all, that is what parents are for. Throughout the animal kingdom, parents instinctively train their young for autonomous survival and then unceremoniously push them from the nest. This function of "launching" is what Kahlil Gibran was depicting when he wrote of the parents' being the bow and the child's being the arrow.

The mature parent and the inner child within all of us often

* Lisa Alther, *Kinflicks* (New York: Knopf, 1976), p. 341.

† *Ibid.*, p. 392.

battle for supremacy in our dealings with our children, and whichever aspect controls our behavior largely sets the tone of the interaction. Let us look at a simple example of how the mature parenting part of the parent and the inner child of the parent may appear in a commonplace incident. Daughter Judy has just announced to mother and/or father that she would like to go to an out-of-town college. Let us suppose that the mature parent in mom or dad thinks this would be fine for Judy's development, but the parent's inner child is fearful of the separation, feeling it as a loss and abandonment. If the mature parent part is in control, the parents may encourage Judy's choice, talk about the practical matters of college selection and finances, and genuinely feel good about it, except for an underlying sad note of wistfulness or nostalgia at the change in their relationship with Judy.

But if the parents' inner child prevails, they might raise all kinds of objections, give Judy the feeling they cannot afford it when they really can, make her feel she is deserting them by leaving, tell her she isn't ready to handle it, etc. And these parents may not be aware at all that it is their inner child speaking but may believe that it is coming from their sensible mature parent judgment.

When the little child within a parent takes over and tries to control his or her offspring, each parent will try to hold on, using methods that he learned as a child and has used since his own children were very small.

For example, if Judy's parents tended to use *guilt* for control, they might indicate, though not in so many words, "How can you go off to school and leave us all alone, particularly when we haven't been feeling that well?" or "Sure you can go. Of course we'll have to stop taking vacations for the next four years, but if that's what you want." If Judy's parents' style of control was to use *fear of their disapproval,* their tone might darkly imply, "If you go to college far away, we'll pay for it, but things will never be the same between us again." If they tended to use *shame* they might say, "I know that you want to get away just to play around. I can't believe that a child of mine could think that way." If *fear of the outside world* was used, they might say, "I hear all kinds of things go on there in the college dormitories that would be bad for you. Why not stay here where it's safe?" If they habitually used *belittlement,* they might say, "You're not mature enough to handle it yet. And you know how you get those asthma attacks when you're nervous."

There are many such techniques parents may use when their adult child is taking a step other than the one which they would like them to take. These techniques are such an integral part of us and so deeply ingrained in us by our own parents that we may not recognize that they are maneuvers aimed at holding on to the old relationship with our children. And if we find ourselves using such maneuvers, we can be fairly sure that our inner child is afraid of the separateness and will use guilt or threats or moralizing to prevent a depressing and frightening gap from growing between ourselves and our children. The child within us, for whom our own offspring have become our parents, dares not let those "parents" get so far away that they won't be available when we feel a need for them.

And our offspring also has his own inner child who harbors all the powerful emotional memories of his own childhood. To a large degree, the inner child of our sons and daughters and our own inner child contain many of the same feelings. *But the aspect of the inner child of our adult sons and daughters that reacts most strongly to their relationship with us has to do with the early conflict of dependence versus independence.* Our children, as infants, went through a prolonged period of almost complete attachment to us. If you are a mother, they came from a oneness with the inside of your body to a near oneness with the outside of your body. Long before they could even know you were separate from them, they turned to you and clung to you to allay their hunger, to calm their fears, to give them comfort. Their dependence was total. Even the word "dependence" is not strong enough to describe the symbiotic fusion and attachment that seems to be the infant's experience. But the need for a safe and blissful merger with you was not the only force at work in your child, because as he grew, his perceptions and his mobility showed him that he was not a part of you, and he seemed both frightened and exhilarated by that discovery. You may recall how thrilled he was when he learned to crawl. Then one day, as he really had it all going for him, with breathless excitement, gasping and giggling, he crawled away from you as rapidly as he could, and turned a corner into another room. And then you heard him howl. You came running, fearing he had hurt himself, but no, he was screaming in terror because once he had turned that corner, he could no longer see you; you were gone. It was as if you had disappeared and he was all alone. You picked him up, and your presence reassured him that he had not lost you, and all was well and secure.

All of these feelings still exist in the inner child of your grown-up son and daughter. On the one hand, there are the feelings that would tend toward dependence on you, such as his need to feel your love, concern, approval, givingness, and being there for him as a secure home base. As part of this dependence, he feels the anxiety and terror of losing your caring and your availability.

On the other hand, there are the feelings that move him toward independence. His inner child as well as his appropriate adult development push him to achieve and maintain his autonomy, to experience and advance his unique strengths and capacities, to move about freely, and to create his own life. Here his fear would be of losing his mobility and separateness, of being forced back into the fusion again, either by you or by his terror of being separate from you. And this portion of the inner child often contains a defiant rebelliousness that is saying, "I will not let my selfhood be annihilated in an attachment to you again."

It is not difficult to see that when the inner child of the parent interacts with the inner child of the offspring, there will be trouble. In fact, *in almost every instance where there is a troubled relationship between a parent and a child, it is because at least one of them, and usually both, are responding in accordance with the feelings and reactions of his or her inner child.* For example, when your inner child, fearful of abandonment, wants greater closeness, and your son's or daughter's inner child (and perhaps their adult self as well) wants greater independence, there will be conflict. And when your inner child (and perhaps your adult needs and parental judgment) wants greater separateness, and your son's or daughter's inner child wants greater attachment and dependence, there will be conflict. These hidden inner-child needs often produce a characteristic way of relating between a particular parent and a particular child. *I call these exchanges between the child within the parent and the child within the offspring Songs and Dances* because they usually come to be performed ritualistically, in an almost predictable and rhythmic manner. The same words, the same music, and the same dance steps are repeated over and over again.

Let's look at an illustrative Song and Dance through a piece of dialogue between a mother (it could easily be a father) and her son (it could easily be her daughter). It begins matter-of-factly enough with the mother's inviting the son to a social gathering at her home and his saying that he is sorry but he had made other plans. We will pick it up from there, with each person's inner child speaking in parentheses. (Actually, the wishes of the inner child are often silent and unrecognized by the speaker. But they do influence the words and tone of what is said.) The mother is responding after her son declined her invitation:

"You can't make it? What do you mean you can't make it? There will be people there whom you haven't seen for ages." (How dare you! You have no right to put other plans before me.)

"I'm really sorry Mom, but I made these other plans a while back." (I hate those parties. But please, Mommy, don't get all upset and angry. When you do, it makes me feel shaky and terrible.)

"You're always pulling something like this. I told everyone you were going to be there. You just have to come." (If you don't do what I want, I'll scream and yell. I may even hold my breath till I turn blue.)

"You shouldn't have told them that without checking with me first." (There you go again, assuming that because I'm your child, you can speak for me and make arrangements for me. I feel smothered. Actually, I don't have other plans, but I won't let you control me all the time.)

"I was sure it would be okay. After all, it's almost three weeks from now." (I'm furious and upset that you're not always available when I want you to be—like when I'd scream for mommy and daddy not to go out but they'd go anyway.)

"Yes, but I've made other plans." (So please don't make that angry witch-face at me. It scares me. I begin to feel like giving in and then I will be just an extension of you.)

"I can never count on you for anything! Everybody else comes first." (I can't stand it that you have a life separate from me when it conflicts with my wishes. It must mean that you care about other people more than me.)

"That's not true. You've counted on me plenty and I've been there. What do you want me to do, drop everything and come running?" (I get all churned up when you act like I'm letting you down. I'm getting so enraged and so afraid I'll give in that I'd like to make you disappear.)

"Oh no. That would be too much to ask. God forbid you should inconvenience yourself for me." (Yes, of course. You should drop everything and do what I want. You're supposed to. If you don't, you're bad.)

"Don't pull that guilt trip on me." (I feel guilty that you think I'm bad, and I'm getting even more angry that you are making me feel guilty.)

"What guilt trip? You wouldn't feel guilty if you missed my funeral. Just wait till you want something from me!" (You don't love me! Well, who cares about you. You'll be sorry.)

"Who wants anything from you? I don't need anything from you!" (You're withdrawing your love! I'm furious. I'd like to smash you.)

"Good. Because you won't *get* anything. And I'll never ask you for a favor again." She hangs up the phone, slamming down the receiver. (He doesn't need me anymore! I've lost him. I'm alone. I'll punish him.)

He calls back. "Look, Mom, don't be so upset. I'll see what I can do to change my plans. If I can, I'll be there." (Please don't be angry, Mommy. I'll do what you say, only stop being angry. Smile at me. Please.)

"Really? That would be so good." (Maybe you really do care. I feel so relieved. And triumphant. You'll be there and everyone will see that you love me.)

"I can't promise anything, but I'll try." (Now I don't feel scared of your anger or of losing your love. But I feel so powerless and so depressed because my fear made me give in. I hate you for making me feel that way.)

"That's all I can ask." (I'm glad you'll try to be there, but if I forced you into it, it still doesn't mean you love me and that makes me sad. And it means I'll have to do this each time I want you to do what I want.)

What can we see in this dialogue? First, we can note how this parent achieved her goal. This mother was angry, even outraged, at the child's refusal to accept the invitation and expressed the anger through her tone, through attempts to command ("You just *have* to be there"), accusations ("I can never count on you for anything"), sarcasm ("God forbid you should inconvenience yourself for me"), guilt provocation ("You wouldn't feel guilty if you missed my funeral"), threats ("Just wait till you want something from me"), and withdrawal of her presence (she hung up).

Her son's responses, although seemingly straightforward ("I'm really sorry, but I made these other plans a while back"), conceal that he doesn't want to be there (I hate those parties), and that he lied about having "other plans." Perhaps this mother, having repeatedly experienced this kind of elusiveness, now senses it is happening again and, smarting from still another rejection, increasingly responds from her inner child. And the son's inner child begins to take over and direct his feelings and words. He becomes more and more vulnerable to being manipulated by his mother's maneuvers and to his own little boy fears of her disapproval, her anger, and her leaving him. These fears alternate with his defiant protest against surrendering his independence by giving in to her. When he does give in, he feels like a defeated and helpless child. These bad feelings will tend to become more pervasive because the seeming success of the Song and Dance assures that, with slight variations depending on the situation, it will be repeated endlessly. Though each may go through the same motions, the emotional base of the relationship will erode, and the potential for a serious rupture, as silently menacing as the San Andreas fault, will always be present. And if the relationship is shattered, each would blame the other, neither one looking at his or her own part in the disaster.

It is probably easy for you to see the Songs and Dances in this illustration because you are not caught up in them. But if you are the parent who is swept up in a frustrated, despairing or angry tango with your son or daughter, you may not have the slightest awareness that the main reason for your being so out of step with each other is that the interplay is between his or her inner child and your own. And without recognizing it as a Song and Dance in which each of you is a partner, your efforts to change it will only have you spinning dervishlike in bewildered and futile circles.

The examples in this book, illustrating the many types of Songs and Dances, are designed to help you recognize whether you are participating in such a routine, because this recognition is the first essential step toward change. It will be relatively easy to recognize your son's or daughter's end of the Song and Dance —you probably suspected all along that he was being "childish." But recognizing your own part in it is another story. There are aspects of ourselves that we'd rather not look at. In his novel *Demian,* Herman Hesse's protagonist says, "I realize today that nothing in the world is more distasteful to a man than to take the path that leads to himself." And the path that leads to awareness of your part in the interplay with your offspring is particularly distasteful because it means that you would have to acknowledge that not all of your motives stem from mature and sensible reasoning but may be prompted by the needy and perhaps demanding little child that exists in you (and everybody). This recognition of the inner child, though often painful, is perhaps most difficult to see when it enters into your role as parent, where you would like to think of yourself as especially wise, benevolent and self-denying. Particularly when there is conflict and your angry children are hurling harsh criticisms and complaints at you, you are almost bound to become defensive and closed, rather than open to an examination of possible truths in their attacking words. At such moments, it is nearly impossible to evaluate coolly whether this is a charge with some merit or is arising out of the unresolved angers of the inner child. Under such stress, it's unlikely you can be objective enough to examine their accusations for nuggets of truth about your end of the Song and Dance. But perhaps afterward, when your blood pressure is back to a less volatile level, you can pan through their words to see if nuggets are to be found there, because they just might prove to be highly valuable to your self-assessment. And this can be a good time to look at what your offspring's inner child may be up to, because you can be sure it was an active participant in the conflict. Maybe with distance, you can discern if your son was right when he accused you of interfering, or if you just simply meant, "How are you?"

After recognizing the part you and your child are playing in the Song and Dance, *the second step is accepting that you can only change your end of the frustrating pattern and not your child's end of it* (only he can do that and he may or may not choose to). In an unhappy relationship, it is always tempting to try to change the way the other person is. I think of a mother who was getting into frequent battles with her daughter because she felt resentful that her daughter didn't call her often enough. She came to the realization that she was bugging her daughter so much about it that it was driving her daughter away. She became aware that she began almost every conversation with an accusation. If her daughter called her she might say:

"Who? It's been so long I didn't recognize your voice."
(or)
"What's the special occasion?"
(or)
"To what do I owe this honor?"
(or)
"You finally remembered I was alive." (or, etc.)

If *she* called her daughter she might begin by saying:

"This is someone from your past. Remember me?"
(or)
"I'm sorry I didn't call all week. I was very sick."
(or)
"I figured if I didn't call you, I might never hear from you again."
(or)
"How come you're always too busy to pick up the phone and call me?" (or, etc.)

This mother saw with sudden clarity that her demanding, guilt-provoking approach was bound to enrage and alienate her daughter. So she took a new tack. When her daughter called, she responded cheerily and made it a point to say absolutely nothing about her not having called more often. She stopped calling her daughter so that her daughter would not feel coerced or smothered. She did everything "right" to avoid the old Song and Dance where she would be accusing and her daughter would respond with hostility. But after about two months of this, she found her own anger growing, because her daughter called no more frequently than before. By the third month, during one of her daughter's phone calls, she found herself saying, "Who? It's been so long I didn't recognize your voice." Her daughter said, "Here we go again," and the mother screamed, "Nothing I do is right. If I call it's no good. If I don't say anything it's no good. You don't care if I'm dead or alive."

What went wrong here? The mother recognized her end of the Song and Dance and tried to act differently, so why didn't it turn out better? One reason is that there was no basic change in the feelings that underlay the mother's Song and Dance, just a change in tactics. While she was trying to be nonintrusive, this did not spring wholly from the adult part of her that wished to see herself and her daughter as two separate people and respected her daughter's need for greater separateness than she'd like, but from the little girl inside herself who was still trying to hold on. So she tried a new ploy, and when it did not work, her underlying need to feel as if she and her daughter were as one surfaced again. In other words, she had tried new variations of the Song and Dance, but under stress she returned to the old steps.

And what about the daughter? She remained caught up in her end of the Song and Dance. The daughter's inner child was still engaged in the old fight for independence, a struggle we must all go through in some way if we are to become mature self-directed adults. But she was so caught up in this conflict that her mother had become the villain of the piece, and she could not recognize that some of her mother's wishes for more frequent contact were not intrusive attempts to take away her freedom but legitimate desires that came out of a long relationship of caring. So the daughter acted as if all mother's attempts at close communications were threats to her freedom, and this frustrated the mother's appropriate parental wishes, as well as inflaming the fears and angers of mother's inner child. With all these feelings surging around inside both of them, it's no surprise that after a few skipped beats, a few new steps, the old Song and Dance would again prevail.

The most important point of this illustration is that since the mother's new way of acting with her daughter was really an attempt to change her daughter's end of the Song and Dance and not her own, it had inevitable failure built into it. It is a paradox that if this mother had gone through a genuine change and felt comfortable about her daughter's calling less frequently, there is a good likelihood that her daughter would eventually see that she was not being coerced and would feel willing and free to call more often. But when a parent's change is an attempt to bring about a desired response in his child, it will almost certainly precipitate a backlash or, at best, a very short-lived change.

Once you've recognized that you are in a Song and Dance and can accept that you can work only on your end of it, you will find that it is still difficult to modify it because that child within you often takes over, overruling your best intentions and firmest resolutions. Your inner child is so certain that if you stop trying to control your children, they will abandon you completely, he is terrified to give up familiar ways of holding on. When your best judgment has led you to feel you should stop a particular unproductive and inappropriate way of relating to your son or daughter, but when you do stop you feel tension or anxiety or depression or anger, you can bet your inner child is taking over. And you will have to find ways of dealing with it so your more considered judgment can prevail. That's the hardest part, because those inner child reactions are planted so early and rooted so deeply. We will be discussing ways to improve the care and rearing of the child within you throughout this book, because the better you can deal with your inner child, the better things will go with your real child.

For the moment, let's assume you've been successful at stopping your end of the Song and Dance. You've recognized that you have been caught up in a futile interaction, you accepted that you could work only on your end of it, and you've dealt successfully enough with your upset inner child to really change your feelings as well as your actions—the melody as well as the lyrics. How would you be different in the relationship with your son and daughter?

You might expect several important changes:

- Since little children see the people closest to them as existing only to satisfy their needs and wishes, if your feelings were *not* controlled by your inner child, you would be free to see your own son and daughter as separate people whose existence is not for the sole purpose of satisfying your needs and wishes.

- Since little children are threatened and frustrated when people closest to them have needs and wishes other than gratifying them (the small child is enraged when mother's attention is not completely at his disposal), if your feelings were *not* controlled by your inner child, you could take more pleasure in your son's or daughter's unique unfolding, even if this meant they had desires, values, and goals that are different from yours.

- Since little children are terrified of being abandoned forever if people closest to them show love, affection and interest elsewhere (the small child's concept of time does not allow him to realize that love can be an enduring feeling despite the focus of loving attention going temporarily to others, nor can he realize that love does not occur in limited quantities so that if others receive some, it need not reduce his share), if your feelings were *not* controlled by your inner child, you would be able to feel secure in your son's or daughter's caring even when their affection and interests focus in other directions.

- Since little children feel that their existence and value is bestowed only by the caring of the people closest to them (the infant cannot survive without that caring, the little child hungers for it to feel secure and worthwhile), if your feelings were *not* controlled by your inner child, you would not need to find your purpose or worth in your son or daughter, but in yourself, and the full living of your own life. Instead of depending on your offspring for your fulfillment and instead of expending so much time worrying about them or being angry with them, your energies could be released to discover and follow your own needs and potentials. For as far as we know, we only live once. That brief span can be made richer and can seem longer lasting by your having as many rebirths as possible. Every time you let go of an old way of being that has outlasted the function it once served, it presents you with the possibility of making a new beginning, and cutting loose from the dependent overinvolvement in your grown-up child offers you just such an opportunity for a rebirth.

As part of this rebirth you can explore what kind of relationship is now possible and would now be most gratifying between your mature children and yourself. Certainly the meaning of giving up old ways of relating that no longer work does not mean giving up on having a relationship with your children just because it's going badly, nor does it mean allowing the relationship to be defined completely by them with your passive compliance. It is much too important for such an abdication on your part. After all, you are a primary source of who your children are, and there are mutual attachments that derive from countless interactions, conscious and forgotten memories, primal needs and profound feelings that go back to their days of oneness with you. You are their roots, and with viable roots they will feel, at any age, less alone, less fragmented and less vulnerable.

And just as you bespeak your children's roots, they are your shoots and branches, your link with all that follows. It is a relationship like none other in its origins, depths and shared experiences. When it goes well, you know what a unique source of joy it can be for both you and your child. When it does not, you have experienced the anguish, despair and disillusionment it can bring. It is worth much for you to succeed in having it go well, and the thrust of this book is to help you improve and gain greater satisfaction from your relationship with that other adult who is your child.

CHAPTER 2

The Music Goes Round and Round

Songs and Dances can be as numerous and diverse as parent-child relationships, but they tend to divide into a few basic themes. Some themes are so frequently heard that a small number, with variations, encompass the great majority of Songs and Dances.

The five most common basic Songs and Dances are:

1. The Guilt Gavotte
2. The Fear Fandango
3. The Shame Shimmy
4. The Hootchy Kootchy
5. The Money Minuet

Let's listen to the melodies and look at the choreography of each of these routines. One or more of them will probably strike a familiar chord.

The Guilt Gavotte

The essence of the Guilt Gavotte is that either you or your child, and most likely both, is trying to control the other by proclaiming, "You are the cause of my suffering, so you owe it to me to make me feel better by doing what I want you to do." In other words, whichever one of you can best prove that you are the victim can claim the victim's right to demand reparations and guilt offerings.

When it is your *grown-up child* who is playing the role of victim, you might hear accusations like these:

"You were always so bossy that I'm afraid to speak up for myself. No wonder everyone takes advantage of me."

"How can you and Dad go away to that convention the last weekend before I go to college?"

"Bill and I have more fights about your visiting us so often than anything else. If we split up, it will be your fault."

"If you hadn't been too busy to spend some time with me when I was growing up, I might not be depressed all the time."

"You wanted me to be a lawyer and I am. But I hate it."

"You made me so dependent on you that I have no confidence or ambition."

"Sure I made a lousy marriage. What do you expect after a childhood of listening to you and Dad fight."

"If you hadn't felt that a career was unimportant for a woman, I wouldn't be stuck in this lousy job."

"You were so critical that I walk around feeling that I'm stupid and worthless."

"How come you can go on a vacation to the Caribbean, but you can't send me more money at graduate school?"

"You always made me feel sex was dirty, and now I'm so hung up that it's wrecking my marriage."

"I know I got married too young. It was the only way I could get away from you."

The truth or falsity of these charges is not relevant. If a parent gets bogged down in trying to set the record straight from his point of view, he will soon find he is involved in a Song and Dance in which his inner child is saying to his son or daughter, "Please don't think those bad things about me. I'm afraid you won't love me." And once he is into that role he is vulnerable to his offspring's demand that he make up for the suffering he's caused by doing what the offspring wants. For example, the grown-up child who said, "You made me feel so dependent on you that I have no confidence or ambition" might add, "so now stop bugging me to get a job," or "so now you should support me till I get myself together." This message would be coming from the frightened or passive inner child of the son or daughter, and if the parent's inner child is too afraid of being criticized or rejected, he may go along with this emotional blackmail and act in a way that serves nobody's best interests.

A parent may be vulnerable to his child's guilt provocations not only because his inner child was partly shaped by his fears of being thought of as "bad," but because of later events as well. First of all, there has been a false but prevalent idea that parents are totally responsible for how their children turn out—for all their child's emotional problems, for his choice of life-style, and for how happy, successful and well adjusted he is. They worry, Did I pick him up enough when he cried or did I pick him up too much? Should I have not worked and stayed home with him more? Did I yell too much? Was I overprotective? Was I too strict? Many parents feel *too* responsible for their child's development, as if theirs was the only influence on the child. In addition, the parents' dissatisfactions with themselves can influence their vulnerability to guilt. One woman who felt that her naiveté and tightness about sex had almost wrecked her marriage was terrified she would pass along her own sexual discomfort and rigidity to her children. She felt confused and guilty whenever she had to face issues about how much permissiveness or structure, how much information and what values she should impart to her children in sexual matters. Since she never felt sure that she was doing the right thing, it was easy for her children to manipulate her by making her feel she was deeply damaging them if she did not let them do as they wished.

If your child provokes guilt as a way of punishing and controlling you, you have probably found the list of typical accusations of the grown-up child familiar. It may be harder to recognize *your own* guilt provocations because, like everyone else, you want to believe that the way you act is reasonable and nonmanipulative. But I'll set down some commonplace *parental* guilt maneuvers, and you see if you can recognize yourself in any of them.

> "I tried so hard to be a good mother and this is the thanks I get."
>
> "I was so sick I didn't think I'd survive. Everyone else took the time to call me."
>
> "If it weren't for you children, do you think I would have stayed in this marriage?"
>
> "What do I care if I come out of the hospital. You'll be better off without me."
>
> "I had nothing to do while you were out, so I washed some of your things and straightened out the room. I hope you had a good time."
>
> "You can't make it? It's okay. I don't mind spending another holiday all by myself."
>
> "With all the money we put into your college and that's the kind of job you take? How can you do this to us?"
>
> "If you marry him, my life is over."
>
> "You can't more so far away. What's the sense of my having children if I never see them?"

If you play the role of victim or martyr, your son or daughter might easily get caught up in one of your guilt provocations and a Song and Dance would be under way. For example, if you make statements such as, "You have time for everyone else, but here I am all alone and you never have time to visit me," the chances are that your offspring will get into either a compliant or a defiant

Song and Dance. If it's *compliant,* he might say, "I'm sorry but I've been working my head off. I'll come by tonight if I'm not too tired," and he may arrive exhausted, resentful and thoroughly unpleasant. If he gets into a *defiant* Song and Dance, he may start screaming at you for "pulling another one of your guilt trips," and avoid visiting for a long, long time.

These bad consequences are likely because built into the Guilt Gavotte is the choreography for a weird conflict, the battle slogan of which might well read, "To the victim belongs the spoils." The winner is the one with the bloodier and more agonizing wounds because he is in position to demand guilty submission. So you and your child could soon be trying to outmartyr each other. If you try to win by making your child feel guilty for not visiting you when you were housebound with a cold, he may tell you he couldn't come because he had a bad migraine. If you tell him the cold has developed into pneumonia, he may tell you he is being checked for a brain tumor. There is an escalation of suffering, each trying to claim the victim's right to control the other, or at least to avoid being controlled by the other. It becomes a sad and hostile mess.

How do you get out of a Guilt Gavotte? First let's look at one in which your son or daughter is making the accusation. Suppose he says, "You were so critical that I walk around feeling stupid and worthless," and he is using that charge to get you to accept a lot of hostile behavior on his part. If the child in you, filled with its own self-doubts and fears of rejection, were to allow this hostility to go on, you would soon become the victim and be provoking guilt yourself. But if you refuse to fall into the guilt battle and look at what's going on from a more adult perspective, you might recognize the hurt and angry child in him and say, "If I was too critical I'm sorry, but attacking me won't help and I don't want it. Let's talk about what you might do to change your feelings of being stupid and worthless." He may still try to make you feel guilty, but if you persist, the gavotte is ended.

What if you're the one making the accusations? If you see the destructive effects of this kind of interaction and want to stop it, the next step is recognizing from where it stems. First, it comes from some frightened and controlling little boy or girl inside you who has learned to use guilt provocation to get his own way. And where did you learn it? Probably from your own parents who may have made you feel you caused them much suffering if you did something they didn't like. The Guilt Gavotte is a dance easily passed from one generation to another. So you have to try to come to terms with your fears that you will be powerless or abandoned if you give up trying to control and your inner child's repetition of your own parents' way of controlling. You have to tune in so sensitively to when you are using guilt that you can hear yourself doing it, and stop yourself, and then reassure the child in you that you'll find better ways of maintaining the relationship with your son or daughter.

The Fear Fandango

A fifty-nine-year-old woman, living in New York City, tells me that she has called her father, who lives in Montana, every Sunday for as long as she can remember. When I asked if she enjoys talking to him she says, "I hate it. And I hate that old S.O.B., but I feel I have to call. It's not obligation or guilt. I'm terrified of him. If occasionally I've had to miss calling him, I get panicky, as if he'll do something terrible."

Her father is ninety-two, frail, forgetful, and semi-bedridden; yet this man invokes all this compelling fright. In actuality, he is powerless to affect her life. He can't even cut her out of his will because he has long ago put his money in irrevocable trusts. So what is the source of her fear and trembling? The source is stored within her, in many "tapes" of when she was a little girl, and his harsh insistence that she behave according to his wishes was backed by rage and severe punishment. That was a long time ago, but all that terror she felt then is also on the tapes, still able to be triggered by the threat of his thunder.

The fear-provoking partner in the Fear Fandango will more often be the parent than the offspring because he or she may have been frightening the child from a time when the child was so young, vulnerable and impressionable that, as with the fifty-nine-year-old woman mentioned earlier, fear becomes an ineradicable part of the child's response. But often enough, the fear-provoker can be the offspring. An aggressive child of any age can often terrorize a household, making the parents ever fearful of his tantrums. These tantrums can be mostly a nuisance when the child is small, but his rages can be frightening as he gets bigger and stronger. Usually as the child gets older, his terror tactics are less physical aggression and more verbal assaults and threats. At times, though, a grown-up child may frighten his parents with violence, particularly if he is prone to alcohol or drug abuse. If you are afraid of your child, you know how vulnerable you can be to his demands. So let's take a closer look at how the Fear Fandango works.

Whether the fear-provoker is the parent or the child, two things will be true:

1. The fear-provoker believes he owns the other person, that the other person is nothing but an extension of his needs and wishes.

2. The fear-provoker will back up his commands with a threatening "or else."

When it is the parent who is provoking the fear, he may baldly express his feeling that his child is his possession by saying such things as, "You're not supposed to think. I'll do the thinking," or "When I say jump, you jump." When it is the child who is provoking the fear, he may express his feeling that his parents are nothing but an extension of him by implying, "You're my parent and you're supposed to do what I want so you'd better." And each has his own "or else" threat. "The (parent's) 'or else' may change as the child matures: 'Or else I'll spank you, beat the hell out of you, stop talking to you, confine you to your room, stop your allowance, throw you out, cut you off, etc.' "* The grown-up child's "or else," as I've indicated earlier, usually is not a threat of physical violence unless he is quite disturbed, drunk or drugged. More frequently he may threaten such actions as "dropping out," not visiting for the holidays, revealing a family secret, moving away, ending all contact, "disappearing," or

* Howard Halpern, *Cutting Loose* (New York: Simon & Schuster, 1976), p. 80. Chapter 5, "The High and the Mighty," gives a detailed exploration of the Songs and Dances invoked by despotic parents.

killing himself. His choice of threat will probably be determined by his knowledge of what arouses most fear in his parents.

The Fear Fandango can have many variations, but the two most common I call "High Noon" and "I Surrender, Dear." First, let's look at how these variations work when it is the *parent* who is the fear-provoker.

Suppose you have long been in the habit of trying to control your child with a self-righteous stance that says, "I am your parent so you better do it my way or else." Often his response (as a child, an adolescent, or an adult) may be a violent rejection of anything you ask of him. Your child has become so determined to show you that he is not an extension of you, not afraid of you, and will not submit to you that he reacts with antagonism to any implicit or explicit threats. You and he are into the variation "High Noon" where any request you make can lead to a violent shoot-out. Your entire relationship may be beclouded by the gun-smoke of this war. You may be feeling the frustration of being furious but powerless.

On the other hand, if your child is responding to your fear provocation with the variation called "I Surrender, Dear," you may feel pleased by his submission. You can then have all the convenience and control of having him respond as an extension of you, almost as if he were an arm or a leg. But be honest with yourself, do you like what he has become? Do you like to see your own child being frightened and spineless? Do you see him as a strong, courageous and self-reliant individual who is well able to handle his life now and after you are gone? If you do not, then your use of fear provocation has caused you to fail at that basic parental job of launching your child. It is time to reconsider your approach. If not, you run the risk that your children will feel, as the fifty-nine-year old woman mentioned earlier said of her tyrannical father, "I can't wait for him to die. For a while I may feel guilty, but then I see myself flying, free!"

Now let's see how the Fear Fandango works when it is the *adult child* who is the fear-provoker. If you have a son or daughter who is holding some threat over your head to compel you to do his bidding, you may have fallen into an "I Surrender, Dear" pattern of appeasement. (For example, the "Send me more money or else . . . " ploy may work to bring about your submission.) But as you have probably discovered, submission will only leave you open to further extortion. On the other hand, if your rage at his demands, his threats and his treating you as nothing but an extension of his wishes has led you repeatedly to reject anything he asks, the relationship may have become a series of High Noon confrontations that can destroy all warmth and caring.

How can you stop the music of the Fear Fandango? It depends on who is the main provoker of the fear. If it is your offspring, you will have to see the motivations of his inner child and the responses of your own. Most likely, the child within your son or daughter is back at a very early age—infancy and the first few years of life—when you did serve, in many ways, as an extension of his wishes. He cried because he was hungry and you fed him; he cried because he was soiled and you cleaned him. That was your role, and when you failed in it, he would become enraged. He also discovered he could scare you, by holding his breath or by running away from you toward a street full of traffic. As he got older and smarter and stronger, he found more ways to scare you, and if this combined with his feelings that you exist to give him what he wants, he began to use frightening threats to coerce you. He may now be adult in years, but the child within him may still be seeing it the same way and acting the same way. If you see that it's just a little kid who is tyrannizing you, you may realize how inappropriate that behavior is for someone your grown-up child's age and conclude that you are doing him no favor by submitting or by fighting it out with him like two kids. You may decide to stop it.

But at that point you may be dealing with the frightened child within yourself. One woman reported that her son had told her that unless she would take care of his children while he and his wife went on vacation, he would ask his corporation to transfer him across the country. ("If there are no advantages to staying here, we might as well move.") When he was a boy and his parents were divorced, this same man would threaten to go live with his father if he didn't get a TV set in his room. These threats always worked then because the mother was too afraid to take a stand that might risk her being rejected and abandoned. So it was not easy for this mother to come to terms with her own inner child to be able to tell her son, as she did, "It would be inconvenient for me to take your kids. If that means you'll move, then you'll move. All I know is that I won't give in to your threats any more." He didn't move, but she couldn't know that beforehand. The risk was real, but necessary to end the Fear Fandango.

If you are the one who is tyrannizing your offspring with fear, you will first have to recognize that you are doing it, and to recognize this you must stop fooling yourself that your child is acting out of "respect" and not fear. Respect is a positive reaction. It requires no demands, no commands, no threats and no anger from you to be elicited. It means your children care about you and admire who you are enough to meet some of your wishes simply because they know it's important to you. As soon as you put an "or else" into it the response you get is not respect but fear.

If you can recognize that you are provoking fear, you next have to see it as coming from the little child in you. You have to see that spoiled brat part of yourself and recognize that such despotic tactics are totally out of keeping with being a mature and loving parent. This means you will have to work on developing the confidence that if you stop throwing your weight around, your children (who may be your parents to your inner child) will not discard you or ignore you. It means having to risk relating to them as peers rather than possessions. That is not easy but will probably have much better results than keeping the Fear Fandango going.

The Shame Shimmy

In the Shame Shimmy at least one of the partners, a parent or his child, is a Saint. It takes no ordination or canonization for him to be a Saint. He doesn't even need religious training. What makes a person a Saint in this Song and Dance is that he believes (in fact, he *knows*) that he is in touch with the absolute *Truth* about how people Should behave. He knows what is the Right way and the Wrong way about every choice, from the most profound moral decisions to what Should be worn for each occasion.

For the Saint there are no shades of gray and little room for personal preferences or predilections as to how a Good Life should be led. If you don't do it his way, the Right way, you Should be deeply Ashamed. And if you are closely related to a Saint, your Bad behavior will bring Shame to him, for which you Should be Ashamed.*

Whether the Song and Dance involves guilt, fear or Shame, the goal is always the same: the person provoking these feelings is trying to *control* the actions of the other. And instilling Shame can be a very strong controller of behavior. Let us suppose that you, the parent, have a touch of the Saint in you. You have strong feelings about how your children Should act in all situations in which you want to get them to do what's Right. You may have heard yourself saying things like this:

> "I never thought a child of mine could do something so Bad."
>
> "Buy the heavier coat. Believe me, I know Best."
>
> "I was so Ashamed when you didn't say a word to anyone," or "I was so Ashamed when you made yourself the center of attention."
>
> "God will punish you."
>
> "Going to a discotheque is a Foolish waste of time."
>
> "Hearing you talk about sex so openly makes me feel Dirty."
>
> "You should feel Guilty for letting your children go out without sweaters on a day like this."
>
> "Family matters must Never be discussed with friends."
>
> "What will People think if they see you wearing those shoes with that dress?"
>
> "Throwing out food is a Sin."

* I capitalize certain words because Saints use words in a very special way, meant to shape the actions of others by setting forth absolute codes of thought and behavior and by providing a system of semantic rewards and punishments to reinforce movements away from the Wrong, Bad and Sinful and toward the Right and Good. There is a Glossary of Saintly Words and Terms in *Cutting Loose*, p. 97. It is part of a discussion on the use of Shame in Chapter 6, "The Saints Go Marching In."

"You Should Never go out to a party when your child isn't feeling well."

"I know I am Right so there's no use discussing it."

If you are prone to saying Shame-provoking things like that, then it is important to realize that the message you are giving your children is that if they do things you don't approve of, though you may still love them (after all, parents Should love their children), you won't Like them or Respect them. And people want to be liked and respected. For children of any age, it is particularly important to feel liked and respected by their parents. So you are transmitting to them a lot of bad feelings about themselves, feelings that lower their self-esteem and self-confidence. A bit further on, we will see if there might not be a better way to guide your children in the development of important values.

Because parents have a primary role in teaching children about life and morality, it is usually the parent who is the Saint in the Shame Shimmy. But sometimes the child can also be a Saint. Perhaps you have heard your child say things like this:

"I was so Embarrassed when you started to dance in front of my friends."

"I can't believe a parent of mine could be such a Racist."

"You follow the religion just when it suits you. What a Hypocrite."

"Why do you have to give in to Dad's Male Chauvinism? You should be Ashamed."

"All you care about is making and spending money. You Don't Care how the rest of the world lives."

"All you care about is saving Money. You don't use it to get any fun out of life."

"I was so Ashamed. Nobody wears their hair like that anymore."

"Act your Age."

"You are so incredibly Narrow-Minded and Old-Fashioned about sex. Can't you see all the harm that approach has done?"

"You make me sick the way you're Afraid to try anything new."

"Sure you're entitled to your point of view, but I've lost all Respect for you."

"I know I'm Right so there's no use discussing it."

When your child is making judgments from on high, trying to make you feel Shame over your behavior and threatening the removal of his liking and respect, it can cause you much discomfort. On the mature parent level, your offspring's esteem is very nice to have. On the level of your inner child, the loss of your son's or daughter's good opinion can arouse fears of losing your connection with him and can shake your own feelings of self-worth.

Whether you are the Saint or your child is the Saint, the Song and Dance you can get into around it has many destructive effects. If you continue to act in ways the Saint disapproves of, it can endanger the relationship and can leave you with an abiding sense of Shame. If you change your behavior, not through conviction or preference, but to avoid the Saint's disapproval, you may be unhappy with your life and feel the weight of being untrue to yourself. Either way, the sooner you stop the Shame Shimmy the better for everyone.

Can you recognize the Saint in yourself? It is not easy because the codes you live by are so deeply ingrained and seem so evidently Right. What makes it particularly hard is that these beliefs may be part of your inner child in that it represents old and powerful learnings taken directly from your own parents. "Did you ever see a kid of about five or six screaming to a friend who is doing something forbidden or daring, 'Don't! My mommy says you should never touch that! I'm going to tell your mommy you did something bad.' There is disapproval, anguish, even horror in the voice of the chastening child. Someone is breaking a parental injunction! Even more, someone is breaking a universal law! This is something wrong, sinful, frightening. It must be stopped."* That upset little child is operating in you every time you feel that you are in touch with the one and only Truth and try to impose

* Howard Halpern, *Cutting Loose*, p. 108.

that Truth on your grown-up children. If you agree that maintaining this stance is harming your relationship with your children and wish to stop it, you will have to take several basic steps.

First, face the possibility that your injunctions may come from your inner child and bring to bear your more mature knowledge, experience and wisdom and try to consider if there may not be other acceptable options.

Second, recognize that your son or daughter is a separate being who may see the world differently and may do things that are different but not necessarily Bad.

Third, realize that while your child will make some choices other than what you believe to be Right, the chances are that he has adopted the great majority of your viewpoints and approaches to life.

Fourth, note that you can continue to like and respect your child even though you disagree with some things he does, and this does not require you to change the beliefs or standards that govern your *own* behavior.

These steps are not easy. I think of Mrs. Wagner, a woman who could qualify as a Saint, who was helped to take these steps by her daughter, Lisa, and thus overcame a seemingly unbridgeable gulf between them. When Lisa got divorced after several years of marriage her mother was horrified. "No one has ever been divorced in our family. I am ashamed to tell people. One should be able to work these things out." But soon she came to accept it as a fact. However, two years later when Lisa began to live with a man she was not married to, it was too much for her mother. "It was bad enough that you humiliated me and shamed yourself with that divorce, but this I will not abide. Your whole life is a violation of how people ought to live. Frankly, I am having trouble thinking of you as any daughter of mine." And she stopped phoning Lisa or spending time with her. After several months of this, Lisa wrote her a letter.

> Dear Mother,
>
> You've really cut yourself off from me and that hurts. I understand it. You feel I've broken with everything you believe in . . . that you've failed with me or I've failed you.

But if you really think about it you'll see it's not true. You have deeply influenced what I believe and how I live each day. I treat people fairly and decently. I am usually honest and aboveboard. And I think I'm kind . . . help people who are in trouble or are needy. I don't exploit anyone. I work hard for what I get. . . . I believe in the fatherhood of God and that He is good and merciful and has created a world of wonders. All these beliefs and many more I got from you.

I am not making light of the two major violations of what you have taught—the divorce and living with Steve. We talked the divorce to death years ago. . . . As for Steve, you stressed that I should learn from my mistakes. I wasn't ready for my marriage and I don't think I'm ready now. I have lots of distrust in my own judgment in this area. . . . Yet I'm a grown woman who enjoys sharing and intimacy with a man . . . so this is a sensible way of handling things for now *and harms no one* (in accordance with perhaps your strongest teaching).

I don't want the choices I've made to stand between us because you mean a lot to me and your being so aloof is punishing and painful. Let's meet for lunch soon. . . .

Love,
Lisa*

Mrs. Wagner was flexible enough to consider what Lisa was saying to her and to shift sufficiently in her acceptance of Lisa to allow her to continue a caring relationship. In fact, the mutual respect for each other continued to grow long after this incident.

Similar principles apply when your son or daughter is trying to make you feel ashamed and threatening the withdrawal of his respect unless you change your way of thinking and being. It is now important for you to point out to him that the two of you are separate people and your values come out of your life's learnings and experiences, which are different from his. And you, too, can emphasize that though he disagrees with some things you do, you are not requiring that he change his views to fit yours. Like Lisa, you can say, "I don't want the choices I've made to stand between us because you mean a lot to me. . . . "

* From a chapter I wrote on the psychology of the expectant heir (Parent-Child Relationships That Affect the Will) in *What's Happening to Your Inheritance* by Martin Levin (New York: Times Books, 1979).

As in ending all Songs and Dances, you will have to assure the child within you that it is not the end of the world if your son or daughter doesn't think well of you and how you are behaving. And it is particularly important to bear in mind that it is often a transitory stage of development for a person to become judgmental with his parents. As Oscar Wilde wrote in *Dorian Gray*, "Children begin by loving their parents; as they grow older they like them; later they judge them; sometimes they forgive them." So your Sainted child's judging of you may evolve into something better, particularly if you stay out of a Song and Dance about it.

The Hootchy Kootchy

Romances between parents and their children of the opposite sex often go on in the family. In fact, such attachments seem to be a normal stage in growing up, a healthy development of the child's capacity to love, to be attracted and to attract. (This romance is part of what Freud called the Oedipus complex.) Usually such a romance has diminished well before the child is out of elementary school and certainly by the time puberty makes such feelings too charged to handle. But occasionally it lasts in some form into the child's adulthood, and then it can stunt his development rather than enhance it.

How does this normal attraction fail to be resolved in childhood? How does it go from being healthy to being destructive? Children are pleasure seeking and affection seeking from the first. They want the comfort and bliss of being touched, stroked and cuddled. We know now that not only do they want it but they need it for their physical and emotional development. Children deprived of it can become withdrawn, ill, even die. Fortunately most parents love their children and like to express this love with tender physical affection. The infant's need to receive affectionate stimulation and the parent's need to give it complement each other beautifully and form the basis of an early reciprocal flow of emotional satisfactions. Starting around age three, the child's desire for this kind of closeness begins to center around the parent of the opposite sex. Little girls talk of marrying daddy, and little boys talk of marrying mommy. But several forces are at work that already point to the end of this romance. First, the feelings themselves may be too powerful for the child to deal with effectively. Second, he is going out into a wider world, meeting more people and new challenges. And finally, his attraction to the opposite sex parent, since he wants her all to himself, puts him into a frightening and unwanted rivalry with the parent of the same sex. Usually, after a few short years he gives it up, almost as if he's saying, "Okay, I can't have her, which is really a relief because it was making me afraid in my relationship with Daddy. But there are others I can be close to and have fun with."

What helps the child most in the resolution of these feelings is if the parent he has a crush on communicates that she loves him very much but is not interested in that kind of relationship, does not want to be possessed exclusively by him or to possess him. This process is particularly aided when the child can see that his parents unmistakably claim each other in a special way, and he cannot be part of that private love.

But suppose a child does not receive those messages? Suppose there is not a close and affectionate relationship between his parents to communicate a natural "off limits." And suppose the parent of the opposite sex encourages an overinvolved relationship with the child, perhaps with sensual and flirtatious overtones. Then the child's own tendency to be possessive and flirtatious is invited to develop rather than dissipate, and the part of him that wants to put away this early romance so he can seek satisfactions in a wider world is undermined. A Song and Dance has begun—one I call the Hootchy Kootchy.

Usually the Hootchy Kootchy has three participants. Besides the involvement of the child and the parent of the opposite sex, there is the other parent who often feels displaced and left out. Listen to the lament of Meg Gordon, a forty-seven-year-old mother.

> Henry adored Sue from the first, and it was one of the most beautiful things you ever saw to watch the two of them together. Sometimes when he visited customers, he would take her with him, and she'd sit in her little car seat pretending she was driving, too. And most mornings he would take her to nursery school. They'd go off hand in hand. I hon-

estly don't believe I was a bit jealous in those years. I loved it. It was the way I thought a father-daughter relationship should be. The way I wish mine had been.

Henry and I began having troubles in our marriage, nothing big, just lots of little irritations. He demands a lot. He's a real get-up-and-go person and always expected me to be ready to get up and go with him. He was annoyed if I was busy with other things, or tired, or just felt like a quiet time at home. So very often Sue would go with him. They'd go horseback riding about every weekend. Sometimes I'd go with them, but frankly, I didn't enjoy it that much and I'm not as good a rider as either of them. The same thing would happen about skiing.

It was when Sue was a teenager that I first noticed myself feeling jealous. It wasn't just those things they did together, but often I felt Henry put those things before being with me and doing what I wanted to do. And at the dinner table at night, I felt like an outsider when they talked. I'd complain about it and they'd say it wasn't like that, that when they talked I was included. Sue said I was supersensitive, and I thought she was probably right, but now I don't think so.

Henry disliked most of the boys Sue went out with. She met Lester in college, and their romance developed so fast that they were deeply involved before we even knew about it. Henry tolerated Lester, but he's not what he would have wanted for her. He's a good man, we both believe that. . . . Henry insisted on helping them with a down payment on a house and had his lawyer handle it. . . . He's there almost every weekend, whether I go or not, and took over the finishing of the basement and putting in a new walk. Many evenings he stops off there first before coming home. . . . You're darn right I'm jealous. I can't get him to move a piece of furniture, and for Sue he moves a whole wall. But it's not just the jealousy, I think it's bad for Sue and her marriage. If I'm jealous, Lester must be even more so. He doesn't say anything, at least not in front of us, but I can sense the tension between them when Henry says he'll be over Saturday to work on the paneling or when he just drops in unannounced. I've had some big fights with Henry about it but he says I'm crazy. And I've spoken to Sue about it. At times she'll agree with me and say she doesn't want to hurt her father's feelings, and other times she'll say I'm crazy, too. But I think it's really that she doesn't want to give up what she has with her father. . . . It stinks. Maybe Lester and I should get married.

Mrs. Gordon's role in this Hootchy Kootchy is a bitter one, and it is easy to see the general destructive effects of this interaction. But why do I refer to it as a Song and Dance? By definition, a Song and Dance occurs when the relationship is largely between the inner child of the parent and the inner child of the offspring. So let's take a closer look at the inner child of each of the participants.

First there is Sue. Though a married woman herself, there is a little girl inside her who adores her daddy the way little girls do. "He's just the biggest, greatest most wonderful Daddy in the world. And look how much he adores *me*. Maybe even more than he loves Mommy. I feel glad I'm beating Mommy out, but I feel sad, too, and scared she'll be angry at me. Sometimes I wish she wouldn't let me get away with it. Maybe it would be better not to be so close to Daddy, but this is too nice to give up."

And then there's the little boy in Henry Gordon. "Sue's so cute. And I love the way she looks at me with those big adoring eyes. And she's just like me, she likes what I like. I love to have people adore me. Especially women. My mother never loved me too much. She never looked at me like that. I mostly feel no one can really be crazy about me. But Sue is and I know just how to keep her feeling that way about me and I don't care what anyone says, I'm going to keep her needing me and close to me and nuts about me."

And the little girl inside the mother, Meg, also does her part in the Song and Dance. "I feel so small and inadequate when I'm with Henry and Sue, just the way I did with my mommy and daddy. My mother was very bossy and my father never really paid any attention to me, so I would feel so hurt and helpless to do anything about it that I'd just withdraw inside myself and get very quiet. I still do that too much with Henry and Sue. It's so hard for me to make a dent with them. I'm still afraid to speak up. I'm afraid they'll both leave me."

Thus the dance between these three little children goes on, seriously eroding Sue's marriage as well as that of her parents, yet none of them is willing or able to stop dancing.

If you recognize that you are in a Hootchy Kootchy, either as a parent overly involved with your child of the opposite sex or a parent who feels left out of the close relationship between your spouse and your child of the same sex, then you have already taken a first step toward ending it. But you'll have to do more than recognize it. You'll have to see how the inner child of each, especially yourself, is deriving benefits from it or repeating patterns from his own childhood. If you are the parent who is overly involved with your child, you have to say to the child in yourself, "Look, you really are adequate and lovable, no matter how your parents made you feel. You don't have to prove you're adequate and lovable by capturing your own son or daughter. You can have a very caring relationship with him (her) without that, and he (she) will love you enough as a parent not to go away. Even if he (she) is in love with someone else and has a closeness with him (her) that you can never be a part of, he (she) will always love you. And you can find your most satisfying love relationship with someone much more appropriate than your offspring."

If you are the parent who feels left out in this Oedipal triangle, you have to check out carefully if you are being overly sensitive to a normal father-daughter or mother-son affection or if there is something going on between them that is too intense, too all-encompassing. If you react to normal closeness on their part with feelings of hurt or jealous anger, you can create the very situation you fear. You may need the help of friends or other objective observers to give you their perspective. If you determine you are overreacting, you must have a talk with your own inner child to see why he is being so possessive and jealous. Are you usually a jealous person? What was the Oedipal triangle like when you were a child with your parents? Did you feel left out? Did you triumph? Are you repeating something from the past or reacting against something from back then? Does your jealousy reflect your doubts about the love of your spouse?

If you check it out and determine that you are indeed the odd man out, then you must ask yourself what contribution you have made to this development. Is your inner child repeating a pattern of being left out from long ago? Is that child too afraid of conflict with your spouse or with your son or daughter? Are you afraid to make waves? Like Meg Gordon, are you so afraid of being abandoned that you are ineffectual in claiming the primary relationship with your spouse?

The Hootchy Kootchy can have destructive effects on so many people—you, your spouse, your child, your child's spouse, your grandchildren, etc.—that it is urgent for you to stop the music by ending the contribution of your own inner child to this melodramatic choreography. Stopping it will send shock waves through the family but can lead to the relationship's becoming more appropriate and comfortable for everyone.

The Money Minuet

It is surprising how many Songs and Dances involve money. What makes it surprising is that since we may think of money's becoming an important part of the parent-child relationship when the offspring gets into adolescence or adulthood, we wonder how feelings and attitudes about money became ingrained in the inner child. But money and the maneuvers around it enter into the interactions of parents and their offspring long before puberty. As an example, I think of the time when one of my daughters was nine years old and came to speak to me about a raise in allowance. She approached me in a very businesslike manner, documenting her expenses and noting the "going rate" among her friends. So I responded in a similar businesslike fashion by asking her what new tasks or chores she intended to do if I were to grant her this raise. "Oh no," she said, "an allowance is not for anything I do, but because I'm your daughter and you love me and you like the way I smile and things like that."

I said nothing more. She got her raise. But more important, I learned something. She was telling me that she considers some forms of giving unconditional, based not on what she did but who she was. In this way she was saying she would not get involved in an interaction with me in which I was trying to use money that in a sense was coming to her (after all, an allowance is not a wage) to control her behavior. If she had gotten involved in such an interaction by specifying new tasks she would undertake, it could soon have led to a Song and Dance, because it would not be long before the child in me would be manipulating with money, and the child in her would be complying or defying.

The history of money between a parent and a child can start long before age nine. You cannot tell if it is a Song and Dance simply by noting if money is given conditionally or unconditionally, because in most instances, parents give some money unconditionally, just because of the nature of the relationship (such as an allowance, birthday presents, school supply money, etc.), and some conditionally, depending on an achievement (such as high grades) or an agreed-upon "wage" for specified work (such as painting the living room). Nor can you tell simply by noting whether there are stipulations as to how it should be spent (it must be put in the bank, can't be used for a toy, may be put toward a car) or no stipulations (it's your money and you can do what you want with it). If you wonder whether you are in a Money Minuet and want to determine if indeed you are, then you must ask yourself these questions:

1. Is your grown-up son's or daughter's approach to you about money in the form of a *request* that comes from his mature assessment of his realistic needs, or is it a manipulative *demand* that comes from his inner child?

2. Is your response to the inner child demands of your grown-up son or daughter based on your most mature parental judgment or from your inner child fears and angers? (I better give in or he won't love me; I'll be damned if I'll give him a cent no matter what.)

3. Is your giving him money and the terms you set determined by your most mature judgment and your caring, or is it the product of your own inner child needs that are trying to control and manipulate him?

4. Is your son's or daughter's response to your inner child's control based on his best adult evaluation of what you want from him, or is it a fearful submission or an unthinking rebellion stemming from his own inner child?

If your answers to these questions indicate that the interaction around money is largely between the child in you and the child in your son or daughter, you can be sure that you are participating in a Money Minuet. And no matter who initiated this Song and Dance, the person who calls the tune can shift back and forth. The choreography of one type of Money Minuet and the way the lead changes is illustrated by Lyman Matthews and his son Arthur. From the time Arthur was born—even before he was born—Lyman was determined that Arthur would go to Yale the way he did. Arthur had little sweaters with a big letter "Y" on them when he was pushed around in his stroller. And starting in the early school grades, Lyman would encourage Arthur's studying by giving him money for high grades on tests and report cards. As Arthur got older, the monetary rewards got greater. Large sums were dangled before him to spur high scores on college entrance exams. No money was given to Arthur for pursuits Lyman thought were frivolous. During the last year or two of high school, Arthur would often ask to borrow his father's car. Frequently, his father would say no, usually with very good reason. Once when Arthur wanted the car for a particularly important date and his father refused, Arthur got very angry, then somewhat depressed, and got the lowest grades on two of his tests that he had ever received. His father was upset and furious, but the next time Arthur wanted to borrow the car, his father gave it to him.

In this way, Arthur discovered that it was not only his father who had power (of the purse) but that he also had power based on his father's wanting something that only Arthur could give him, his success at Yale. Once Arthur was attending Yale—where he was admitted readily—and he asked his father to buy him a car for use at college, he had only to mention that it was so *depressing* not to be able to get around, and a car was practically on its way. Who was controlling whom? It's like the old cartoon of the rat in the experimenter's cage saying, "I have this guy really conditioned! All I have to do is press the lever and he sends in a food pellet."

If we look closely at the interaction between Lyman and his son, we see Lyman's inner child at work, first of all in his *expectation* that Arthur would certainly attend Yale. We must differentiate between a parental preference or wish and the type of *expectation* that grew out of the little boy in Lyman who saw Arthur not as a separate person, but as an extension of his own needs, or even of his own self. Lyman then used money to get what all children want, his own way. The child within Arthur also wanted his own way and discovered his father's vulnerable spot, which he could maneuver to meet his own wishes.

I know Lyman and Arthur now, years after Arthur graduated from Yale, and the Money Minuet still goes on between them about bigger issues and bigger dollars. Arthur is a vice-president in his father's business. He is always threatening to leave the business if things are not done his way. His father is always implying that if Arthur leaves the business, he can forget about his inheritance. These bitter maneuvers have squeezed real love, caring and respect out of their interaction, leaving a corpse of a relationship, a mummy preserved with wrappings of dollar bills. What a sad development, but one that was inevitable when neither father nor son took steps to end the Song and Dance.

As we have seen, it is often difficult to determine who started a particular Money Minuet because the tune-caller can shift back and forth from the earliest days. Is the initiator the little child who gets his parents to give him what he wants by saying such things as, "You've got to get me Adidas sneakers because all the other kids are wearing them and I'll be left out"? Or do his parents start it by having made the child aware that they are overly concerned that he have friends and they would be terribly upset if he were left out? So while it is difficult to determine just how it gets started, there are certain situations and moves that can easily act as invitations to a Money Minuet between a parent and an adult child. Here are some invitations that typically may be proffered by a grown-up child:

> "We'll never have a chance to buy a house like this again. We can swing it if you lend us the down payment. We're not sure when we can begin paying it back or if we'll be able to afford any interest on it."

> "You've got plenty, so what's it to you to give me a little seed money to start my own business? Don't you want me to get ahead?"

> "I know I went in over my head, but I thought I could count on you to bail me out if I couldn't handle it. You always used to."

To the extent that these statements are coming from the little child part of the adult son or daughter, they can represent his end of a potential Money Minuet. If you respond from your inner child, a Song and Dance is under way. For example, the parents of the young man who asked for "seed money" to start a business knew that he had never reliably stayed with anything, had no business experience, was always looking for an easy buck, and had not thoroughly investigated the business opportunity he was contemplating. Yet his father felt vulnerable to the son's insinuation that he did not want him to succeed, and the mother hoped that this would give her son just the push in the right direction that he needed, and both parents were afraid of being seen as unloving, so they gave him the money. In other words, the insecure inner child of each took over instead of their best judgment, with results that could be predicted. Their son blew the whole thing, deepening his own feelings that he's a failure and once again disappointing and angering his parents. It would have been better had they said, "I'm sorry, but in our judgment this is a bad venture and we won't support it. It would be bad for all of us. If you get yourself some business experience and show that you can be reliable and consistent, we would be happy to help you get started at that time." They would have avoided involvement in the Money Minuet. The son's furious inner child may have continued to try to draw them into it by accusing them of not caring, by threatening to stop seeing them, or whatever. But if the parents maintained a mature parental stance, caring but not easily manipulated, the long-range results would likely be much better.

Now let's look at some invitations to a Money Minuet that parents may give their adult children.

> "I haven't taken a vacation in years or refurnished the apartment because I've wanted to leave more for you. But why should I when you can't even spend Christmas with us?"

> "I don't want you living in that neighborhood. Why don't we buy a co-op apartment for you in a nice building in a safe neighborhood. We'll own it, but for all intents and purposes it will be yours. Maybe Dad and I will stay over occasionally if we come into the city for the theater or something."

"I'll be happy to lend you the money for the house but not for the adjacent lot. I know you'd like to have the extra space so I'll tell you what . . . I'll buy it myself and you can use it any way you want."

"Your sister married a decent man and is leading a decent, normal life. Whom do you think I'm going to leave my money to, you or her?"

To the extent that these statements represent an attempt to control by the parent, then they reflect a maneuver by the child within the parent to hold on to and manipulate his son or daughter. If the child in the offspring gets involved with it, then round and round they will go in this exhausting minuet. For example, the young woman who accepted her father's offer to buy the lot adjacent to their house was to have many regrets about it, as did her husband. Dad began to talk about how nice a small greenhouse would be on one corner of that lot, how instructive it would be for the grandchildren (his hobby was horticulture). He put so much pressure on them, they let him build it (after all, it was his property). And so there was dad every chance he got, puttering in the greenhouse. The sense of being on their own that this couple wanted was frustrated. They became so bitter about it, they wouldn't offer him a chair or a cup of coffee when he came by. He felt hurt, unwanted and perplexed.

If you want to end or stay out of a Money Minuet, the primary prescription is, as always, keep your eye on when the inner child is trying to gain control and don't let it happen. Some general guidelines about money and your adult offspring can help you to do this.

1. Your money is your money and you are under no obligation to give it or lend it to any of your adult children.

2. If you choose to give or lend money to your child, it is a choice that should arise out of your parental love, your personal values, and your most realistic assessment of his monetary situation and your own.

3. It is important in responding to your grown-up child's request for money not to respond to any demands and ma-

nipulations of his inner child with the needs, demands, fears and manipulations of your own inner child.

4. If any arrangement is made for a sizable or regular sum of money to go from you to your grown-up son or daughter, the terms and obligations of each person should be explicit, clear and mutually accepted.

5. If money is given, clearly specify whether it is a loan or a gift.

6. If the money granted is a loan, the terms must be spelled out. How much? For how long? When does repayment start? Is there interest? Exactly how is the interest to be calculated?

7. If the money granted is a gift, there may still be conditions ("I'll be glad to give you money to go back to school," or "Here's $2,000 toward a new car"), but these stipulations, too, must be explicit.

8. Whether the money granted is a gift or a loan, there must be no *hidden* strings attached, such as "I gave you money for a car and you never take me anywhere with it" (unless taking you somewhere was an explicit and accepted condition of the gift), or "I lent you money to buy the house and now you hardly ever have me over" (unless having you over on some regular basis was an explicit and accepted condition of the loan). Certainly your child's seeming lack of consideration when you've been generous is galling and upsetting, but adding stipulations later that previously had existed only in your own unexpressed expectations is almost sure to cause a lot of trouble.

9. You have the right to ask for whatever conditions you wish if you grant money to your grown-up child. Make such conditions reasonable, meaning that they come from your adult needs rather than your inner child needs. For example, it could be considered reasonable to say, "If you want me to lend you $15,000 for a down payment, I want the right to see the house first and give you my opinion on it. If I think it's a bad deal, I have the right to say no because I don't like to get involved in bad deals." But it might be considered unreasonable (and an inner child demand) if you say, "I'll lend you the $15,000 provided you have us over

every Sunday," or ". . . if you let me decorate the house," or ". . . provided the house is right down the block."

10. One type of condition you cannot put on any loan or gift is that your child *love* you, or *like* you, or *want* to spend time with you, or *want* to do certain things for you. You may require him to *do* certain things, but you cannot require that he have the *feelings* you wish him to have. Those feelings are a product of the total past and ongoing relationship.

11. If you have agreed to pay for college or graduate school for your child, the terms of that should be very clear beforehand. Is making such payments something you consider a proper parental responsibility, or are you giving a gift, doing a favor or making a loan? Are there conditions as to what college he must attend, what grades he must maintain, and what course of study he must take? If so, these conditions must be set forth beforehand or there may be too much latitude for a Money Minuet to begin.*

12. In making your will, keep in mind that you do not owe it to your child to grant him any or all of your estate or to divide the money equally among your children. You don't have to give money to someone you don't like or for possible uses you don't like even if he is your child. And you have the right to name the terms that would make him eligible to receive a legacy (that he must be married, be a church-goer, or whatever). But if you are going to withhold an inheritance from your child or make such stipulations, then you must be very sure that your decision is arising from your adult values, judgments and preferences, and not from your inner child who is planning to punish or control your children from beyond the grave simply because they were not being the way you wished they would be.

13. It is inviting a very destructive Song and Dance to use the promise of a legacy or the threat of disinheritance to control your child's behavior. Such promises and threats

* In his book *How to Stop Worrying About Your Kids* (New York: Norton, 1978), J.D. Sanderson shows how he and his wife designed an approach to make their children independent adults at eighteen. This meant that they had to be completely self-reliant at that age, including taking care of their own college costs. He shows how it can be done and the positive effects it had on his children.

can, however, sometimes bring about the behavior you want. (For example, "Now that I'm old you take me into your home or I'll cut you out of my will" can keep you out of a nursing home, but you will have to judge if it's worth the trade-off in bad feelings.)

14. You are probably entering a Money Minuet if you frequently and consistently deprive yourself materially in order to give money to your adult children in the present or in the future through a legacy. The chances are that the motivation comes from your inner child who is saying, "Look how good I am! See how much I love you? See how much I sacrificed for you? Now do you appreciate me? Now do you love me?"

15. You have *no* right to tell your adult child how to spend his own money whether he's earned it, saved it, or inherited it. If he wants to buy a Porsche with his last cent, or sail around the world, or invest it in soy beans in Antarctica, you can tell him your views about it, but it's his decision and he knows his own priorities and will have to live with the consequences. If you try to tell him how to spend it or are punishing him in some way because you don't like what he is doing with it, you'll find yourself in a Money Minuet before you can say Wolfgang Amadeus Mozart.

The Money Minuet can take so many forms that only a careful scrutiny of your interaction with your child about money, now or in the past, can help you discern if you are doing that dance. But these guidelines should give you a basis for getting out of one or staying out of one.

Stop the Music

There are many other Songs and Dances but most derive from the basic five: The Guilt Gavotte, Fear Fandango, Shame Shimmy, Hootchy Kootchy and Money Minuet. You may find that you are in a combination of two or more. The Money Minuet, in particular, can easily combine with many of the others. If you are unhappy with what's happening between you and your grown-up son or daughter, let yourself think about these Songs and Dances, and let yourself confront the possibility that you are engaged in your own particular version of any of them (or of one that I may not have mentioned here, but where you can see that the interaction is between the inner child of your offspring and your own inner child). If you see what you are into, it will be easier to move the relationship to a more adult-to-adult level. As one mother put it, "I was always feeling upset and angry with Deborah. It was making me sick. We were like two children always blaming and trying to make the other one look like the bad one. Blame, blame, blame. I got sick of blaming and sick of being blamed. I felt it just wasn't worth living that way. Then I decided, Okay, I am me and she is Deborah and either we have a grown-up relationship or we don't have any relationship, but no more blame games. I never was able to stop the blame games with my own parents—we were always accusing each other of letting each other down—but I was determined not to do it anymore with Deborah once I saw it. I wouldn't respond to her blaming me and I gave up blaming her. I just said to myself, No, I won't do it anymore. Sometimes I had to bite my lip. . . . Once she accused me of harming her by always treating her like a child. I almost answered 'You act like a child' and telling her she lets me down. But I could see so clearly what would happen that I bit my lip and heard myself saying something like, 'I'm sorry. I'll try not to do that.' It felt so strange to say that, and so good. Deborah didn't know what to say. . . . After a while things began to change. We talk differently. It's less intense; we're not in each others guts, but I think it's closer."

She had stopped the jangling and exhausting old Song and Dance (their "blame game" was their version of a Guilt Gavotte) and made a place for a new harmony.

CHAPTER 3

Don't Blame Me

"Why is he so angry at me?"

I've heard variations on this question asked hundreds of times by parents of grown-up children, and what strikes me is not only the hurt and bewilderment, but the anger in the voices of the parents. Their child is angry at them, and they are angry at their child's hostility. A relationship that they hoped would be close and warm is filled with harsh words or silence, with accusations or avoidance, with fire or ice.

Sometimes the sharpest thrusts of the anger go toward one parent, sometimes toward the other, often toward both. But the content of that anger, the accusations that are hurled, usually have differing roots, depending on whether the anger is directed at the mother or father. If you are the *mother* of an angry grown-up child, you need ask yourself, How did a relationship that began with such incomparably intimate and caring involvement in each other's lives deteriorate into so much resentment, even hatred? How did I become a participant, maybe even a casualty, of a battle I never wanted?

The answer, in part, lies in understanding what a mother's role is—whether it be your mother or you as mother. Mother is our origin, our lifegiver, our primary source of nurturance and security and warmth. Though we may live to be a centenarian, though our mother has had little actual place in our lives for years, though she may have been dead for decades, as the primeval harbor and primal lover, she resides in our neurons, in those numberless unremembered but ever-influencing memories from infancy on. Is it any surprise that on a hospital ward where people of any age lie in pain and fear, you can frequently hear them cry out "Mama"?

Otto Rank, an early psychoanalyst, saw much of the drama of life as arising from what he called the birth trauma.* It isn't necessary to accept the literalness of Rank's theory (and indeed there is little concrete evidence to support it) to be impressed by its metaphorical truth. For him, the universal experience of leaving the warmth and serene security of the womb to be thrust out into the world is an event both terrifying and indelible. We want to go back where it's safe and comfortable. But there is an another force, a life force, that propels us to grow and distance ourselves from this warmth. This life force tells us that to go back to the womb once we have left it is a kind of death and generates a fear of losing our selfhood and everything that makes us vital, breathing, separate individuals. So we move forward again, away from the womb, and re-experience the birth anxiety, the *life fear* of a world filled with unknown perils, startling stimuli and the necessity of making choices. We pendulate between these two goals, and how we do that defines, in large measure, who we are.

While there is little concrete evidence to sustain a specific birth trauma theory, the clinical and experimental observations of a host of researchers in early development do support the observation that the child's earliest needs are for as perfect a fusion as is possible with mother, and while never fully relinquishing those needs, he moves away into wider spaces and toward increasing self-reliance.† But you need not consult the theories and the re-

* Otto Rank, *The Trauma of Birth* (New York: Brunner, 1952).

† Some of the most important contributions in this area have been made by John Bowlby, *Attachment* and *Separation* (New York: Basic Books, 1969); Margaret Mahler, *On Human Symbiosis and the Vicissitudes of Individuation* (New York: International Universities Press, 1968); and Rene Spitz, *The First Year of Life* (New York: International Universities Press, 1965).

search. Look no further than yourself as a child and adolescent and the development of your own sons and daughters to see the struggles between that magnetic pull toward the safety of the old dependence, on the one hand, and the lure of the risks of being self-directed and autonomous on the other hand. And you are doubtless well aware of it in your current adult lives, for it is a conflict from which we are never completely free. Should I leave the familiar safety of being a homemaker, even though it's no longer very satisfying, for the unfamiliar terrors of getting a job? Should I leave the familiar security of my marriage for a new and unknown way of life? Should I leave this place where I've lived for so many years to risk life in a new locale? Back in the 1950s, when I was a staff psychologist at a Veterans Administration Hospital, many of the professionals would talk at the lunch table with both excitement and anxiety about leaving our secure government jobs for the financial and emotional hazards of private practice. We would talk of it in terms of whether we dare to chance leaving "Mama VA," and we could feel the opposing forces at war within us.

For your sons or daughters, when they were infants and young children, this universal *internal* conflict inevitably was played out primarily *in their interaction with you*. In their infancy, they needed to feel your ubiquitous presence, your closeness, your love, your protection, your touch, your nurturing. They couldn't get too much of it. And you couldn't give too much of it. Your adoring symbiotic tie to your child in that period was his sunshine, milk and vitamins. But as he or she grew, and if you were sensitively tuned in to his signals, you could see his need to become mobile and willful and separate, and you supported that need in accordance with your best judgment of what he could handle. In other words, you helped your child to move away from you. As Nancy Friday wrote, "The primary rule is that a mother can't go wrong, ever, by encouraging her child after age one and a half to be as individuated and separated as possible."* Your child's separation proceeded gradually, with his moving away, coming back for reassurance, and moving away again, perhaps a

* Nancy Friday, *My Mother, My Self* (New York: Delacorte, 1977), p. 60.

bit further. Each step was frightening to your child, and he needed your backing to take these steps toward independent functioning.

Since your child's internal conflict between symbiosis and separation was present in his daily interaction with you, you have been the butt of all the anger and blame that arises out of his bouncing back and forth between these two opposing drives. Sometimes you have deserved this anger, because of your own failures to be sufficiently sensitive to how much dependence and how much relinquishing of your control in support of his independence was needed at any given time. Sometimes you have *not* deserved the anger, but your child projected his own internal conflicts onto you, as when a little boy I know decided, after much inner struggle, not to go on a weekend trip with his class and later griped to his mother, "You never let me go anywhere." It is difficult for a parent to discern when the gripe is just and when it is a projection, but it is wise to assume that if your offspring is an adult and is still frequently making such accusations, you have something to do with it or at least haven't found a way to make the accusations stop.

If we bear in mind the two contradictory developmental needs of the growing child, attachment and autonomy, it is not surprising that the two categories of complaints that mothers most frequently hear from their adult children could be headed: You Bother Me Too Much and You Don't Love Me. The first, arising from the need for separateness, is saying that you're too close, controlling, intrusive and smothering. The second, coming from the need for closeness, is saying the opposite—that you are distant, uncaring, selfish and insensitive. At times, you may hear both of these conflicting accusations from the same child, depending on the situation. But usually your child's complaints will fall into one category or another.

You Bother Me Too Much

You probably remember the television commercial of several years ago with the exasperated daughter saying, "Mother, please! I'd rather do it myself." And perhaps you can still see the look of hurt and puzzlement on the mother's face. More important, you may have heard similar words from your children and reacted with your own pain and confusion. You have heard yourself say, "I was only trying to help—concerned about how you were—wanting to say hello—worried if you got home okay—interested in what you decided—wanting to give you my advice—telling you how I feel. . . ." You say, *I was only* because that's how it feels, like what you did or said was a small thing and meant no harm. You are apologizing for an action that seemed to you natural and right but to which your child is reacting as if it were a malicious transgression.

When your child is responding with any form of "You bother me too much," you can be sure that your needs for a close tie and his needs for separateness are out of phase at that moment. If you hear this a lot, then this is more than a momentary out-of-phaseness. It may indicate that your basic position about the relationship and the position of your child are truly different, making clashes frequent and inevitable.

It's sometimes helpful to see how a problem works by looking at an extreme example. Mrs. Jerney, a middle-aged woman in a Boston suburb, spoke to me briefly by phone on a radio show. I arranged to speak to her again later because our first conversation was limited by the time requirements of the program. "I have a daughter. Or should I say I *had* a daughter? When she was small we were very close. She'd rather be with me than with anybody. Then, when she was fourteen, my husband died, and about a year later, we began having trouble. She wanted to be out all hours and didn't want any responsibility. At first I was easy because I knew she took her father's death very hard. Besides, he did the disciplining, and I wasn't used to it. But then I felt I had to put my foot down. I couldn't stand the way she was acting. I had worked hard to bring her up in a good Christian home, clean and neat and respectful, and here she was, acting like a tramp and keeping her room like a pig pen. The more I tried to get control, the more she would battle.

"When she was seventeen, she took off and went to Colorado with some guy to be a ski bum. I was terribly sick at the time, with arthritis, and really needed her help, but she left a note saying she had to make her own life and just went. She called from out there, and we screamed at each other, and I never heard from her for six years. No calls, no letters, nothing. I knew where she lived and wrote to her from time to time. Then it turned out I had chronic leukemia and some other illnesses besides the arthritis. The doctor told me I'd need some help, so I managed to find her phone number and called. I told her I couldn't work anymore, and I was afraid I couldn't pay for the house, and it would be taken away. She told me she was sorry, but she believes in separating from parents! I was desperate. I pleaded with her and cried, and she just blew up and screamed about how I always tried to ruin her life, and then she said, 'I don't care if they come and drag you up the street on your ass! I'm not coming back, and I'm not sending you a dime.' That was five months ago, and I haven't heard from her since. You can't tell me I ever did anything so bad to her to be treated worse than a dog. What's wrong with her that she has no feeling?"

Well, what is wrong with her? Why is this daughter acting in such a callous and vicious way? It is as if her inalienable right to become a person separate from her mother has gone haywire, has run berserk in ways that eliminate all compassion and concern. The angry and defiant child within this grown-up daughter has taken over so completely that she now becomes as incensed at any interference with her doing what she wants as does a small child who is told she must go to bed instead of watching another TV show. Her rage blinds her to her mother's legitimate needs and obliterates any sense of responsibility. She feels her mother's requests as a dangerous and unacceptable assault on her autonomy that she must resist at all costs.

Why has this normal need for independence run so amuck? There is no way to know for sure, in this particular instance, on the basis of the scant and one-sided information provided. But I know some of the reasons that I have often found to be present when there is so much anger. In part, these reasons can be seen in the *social context* of the relationship. Here is a girl who picked up at age seventeen and moved far away with a man to whom she was not married, became a ski bum, and angrily severed all ties with her mother. In Mrs. Jerney's youth, this would have been unthinkable. But in the years since Mrs. Jerney was seventeen, there were enormous changes brought about by the various social revolutions—youth culture, the women's movement, the sexual revolution, and a general emphasis on living one's life more fully and freely that often was carried to an extreme of smashing established practices and denying commitments.

Mrs. Jerney's daughter was a child of this period of shifting values, as is true of many of you who now have adult children. These changes, which perhaps have forever altered many social expectations, greatly influenced this girl's choices and actions, even if only in making them feel more permissible. But they do not explain these choices and actions, because many children raised in this same social matrix made different choices. We have to look to the nature of her early relationship with her parents, particularly her mother. We note that Mrs. Jerney said, "When she was small we were very close. She'd rather be with me than with anybody." Did Mrs. Jerney keep her daughter so close for so long that this girl developed no awareness of her mother as a separate person with needs of her own, and no sense of caring, no concern to be responsive to those needs? This may have happened because we know that when mothers and children have a prolonged symbiotic attachment, the child can begin to see mother as a tool, as a service station, as a need gratifier and not as a person in her own right. We also know that when the attachment has been prolonged, the child becomes overly centered in his own continued and immediate pleasure with little capacity or desire to delay his gratification ("I want it now and you must give it to me"). And even though his mother's holding him too close too long gives the child the satisfaction of having that personal service station, the part of her child that wants separateness would feel mother as so suffocating that he would be in a state of continual revolt, ready to flare into an insurrection at the slightest threat of smothering.

We see also that Mrs. Jerney had taken a passive position in her daughter's growing years, preferring her husband to be the rule setter and disciplinarian. After her husband's death, there was little structure for her daughter, and when Mrs. Jerney tried to set limits, she was behaving in a way that was alien to herself and infuriating to her child. This woman had built up no backlog of respect to call on in this new position of sole parent.

What was the inner child of this mother like that made her so possessive and yet so ineffectual? I would imagine that as a little girl, Mrs. Jerney had practically no confidence that she could be loved for who she was but found that she could at least keep people close by being of service to them. So she was probably helpful to her parents, striking up the unspoken bargain that as long as she was good, they wouldn't leave her and would, in fact, take good care of her. And being good meant she was not to develop her own unique strengths and desires if these conflicted with her parents' expectations. Because she believed that being dependably of service was the ticket to sustaining loving closeness, the inner child of Mrs. Jerney tried to strike up the same bargain with her daughter. But it didn't work. Instead of holding her daughter to her, it contributed to her daughter's becoming too selfish and rebellious to be there for her mother when her mother, in extreme need, reached out for help.

Most mother-child conflicts of the You Bother Me Too Much type are less severe than this probably irreparable rupture between Mrs. Jerney and her daughter. But a similar, though more muted, Song and Dance may occur whenever the underlying theme is that at this particular moment of the conflict, the mother's needs for more frequent, more involved or warmer contact are opposed by her child's wish for more distance and less involvement.

Let's look at a commonplace mother-child interaction. Daughter is setting up her own nest and establishing a life apart from her parents. Perhaps she has married or has moved into an apartment by herself or with a roommate. Mother wants to talk to her on the phone several times a week and help her shop for home furnishings. Daughter is resisting these requests by her mother. Mother is hurt and angry. Daughter is angry and guilty. Some form of this scenario is probably occurring in every city apartment house and on every suburban block on any given day.

If we look closely at the mother, we see that part of her reactions stem from her "appropriate adult requirements" of the relationship. She loves her daughter and wishes to be of help. She wishes to offer her larger experience and knowledge in this new phase of her daughter's life. She has an understandable desire to retain a caring continuity of this special relationship. But there is also the inner child speaking in the mother. This inner child is saying, "Don't you know that you are an extension of me? That I can't stand it when you go away from me and have a life separate from me? It makes me feel discarded and abandoned. It makes me feel you don't love me anymore. And that hurts terribly. And makes me furious." Both these aspects of the mother, the mature parent and the inner child, coexist and intermingle so that it is hard for the mother or her daughter to know which is speaking most loudly at any given moment.

Now let's look at the daughter. Her "appropriate adult requirements" are clear. She is at the point of taking one of those landmark steps toward independence and self-reliance. She needs to feel that she can manage her own life. She needs to test out and discover what she can do as an adult. It is in keeping with this developmental step that she must de-emphasize ties with her mother of the same frequency and nature as previously. Her assertion of this is important and healthy. But then there is the child within her who is afraid of the hazards of these growth steps, who feels the wish to go back where it's safe and who then rebels defiantly against that wish and against all who would seem to tempt her or coerce her to go back to being the dependent baby. That inner child is furious at any attempt to maintain ties she is trying so hard to loosen. To that child, almost any request for contact can seem like a trap, an enveloping and deadly plastic bag thrown over her attempts to breathe free. So that child is not reasonable, cannot see that she can maintain ties with mother and be separate, too. In a rage, she fights for her life and mother is the enemy.

What can you do if you are caught up in this kind of interaction with your grown-up child? It helps to listen closely to your offspring and hear both his appropriate adult requirements and the voice of his inner child. But what helps even more is to get in touch with those different voices in yourself. You can assume that part of your reaction, perhaps the far greater part, comes from your appropriate requirements as parent. But what about your inner child? Can you hear that part of yourself? When you ask your son or daughter to be in much more contact than he obviously wants, can you discern the part of you that is a little girl afraid of losing him? Of being abandoned? Of being overlooked? Of being forgotten? Sometimes you can hear that little girl in the tone of your voice. Does it get high pitched and whiny? Strident and demanding? Imploring and uncertain? Your most telling clue that it might be the little girl inside you may be in the feelings in your body. Do you feel fear clench your stomach or your gut? Do you feel a sad longing fill your being? Do tears swell in your head and push against your eyes? Does rage quicken your breathing and push you toward a tantrum? These are the kinds of body signals which can tell you that it is probably the little child in you and not your adult requirements that is pushing you toward participation in a Song and Dance.

That recognition of your own inner child is a big part of being able to stop your end of the Song and Dance, because then you know that you are not reacting solely from rational motives. If you can take that step, perhaps you can take the next step of reassuring the little girl *inside yourself* that she is not being abandoned and ignored, that it really isn't catastrophic if your offspring needs more distance. And from that wider perspective, you can look at your daughter and see that there is a little girl in her, defiantly and belligerently engaged in the unresolved old business of being independent from you, and perhaps that recognition will arouse the mature parenting part of you to support the effort. You will also see the appropriate and legitimate requirements of your daughter as a young woman who has achieved considerable self-reliance and therefore needs fewer lines of contact with you. Perhaps this will arouse your prideful respect and allow you to pat yourself on the back for doing well in the parental job of launching your child.

With these steps taken, if you can stop reacting from your own demanding inner child and allow this mature parenting part to dominate, perhaps you can communicate your appropriate, legitimate wishes in a direct but undemanding and uncoercive way that is much more likely to improve rather than inflame the relationship.

Let's go back now to the example of the daughter who is angry because her mother wants her to call too often and wants to help her shop for furnishings. Let us suppose that this mother, having extricated herself from the Song and Dance by recognizing and refusing to respond from her own inner child, were to say to her daughter, "I can really understand that you need more distance from me to establish your own place and feel your independence. And I respect and value that. Sometimes I may get too demanding because I guess I'm afraid you're growing away from me and I'll lose you. But aside from my inclination to hold onto you because of my fear, I do love you and want us to be a part of each other's lives. Perhaps we can figure out together how often and in what ways we can be together that will be satisfying to us both."

It doesn't have to be those words as long as it's that melody. You can see that if you made this kind of statement, it would be coming from a different place in you, and it would be inviting your daughter or son to a whole new level of relationship, perhaps better than ever before. Whether, and how soon, your offspring will be able to pick up on your invitation will depend on her ability to recognize and not respond from the defiant child within herself. There is no magic here. It won't automatically make her say, "Wonderful, Mother. I'm glad you appreciate where I'm at. Now, let's say we call each other once a week and have dinner together every two or three weeks." She may have a long way to go before resolving her own conflicts enough to respond positively to this new situation. But whether she does or not—and probably after a while she will—the important thing is that you have changed, and this change will mean that less of your energies and preoccupations will center around your child, freeing you to be the separate person you were born to be long before your offspring emerged from you into the world.

You Don't Love Me

I know a thirty-nine-year-old woman who had recently been divorced and was moving from a large house to an apartment with her two children. None of the financial arrangements for the sale of the house or the divorce was completed, and she had very little cash. She needed about $2,500 for the costs of the move and for the security and rental for her new apartment. She asked her mother, a widow, for a short-term loan. Her mother said that she was having "cash flow" problems and couldn't do it. There was ample evidence that her mother had considerable means.

"At first I couldn't believe it," the young woman said. "And then I realized, of course, this is nothing new. She's never been there for me. As a child, I could never really talk to her about feelings or be comforted when I was sad. She always seemed to have good reasons for not being there when I was in a school play or something. When I took an apartment of my own after graduation, she was too busy to help me with the move. When I tried to speak to her about my troubles in my marriage, she seemed more upset about how a divorce would look than about my unhappiness. So why should I be surprised now. She's never come through. I don't believe she really loves me."

If you've been getting this kind of message from your son or daughter, ask yourself, Is this is a maneuver and a distortion based on your offspring's inner-child demand that you always meet his needs? Or is there truth in it? Have you had difficulty being there for your child? Do you have trouble being giving? These are difficult questions for any mother to answer for herself, but you can actually address yourself to them. And perhaps you can risk asking others who know you well and will answer honestly how they see you on this score. Not every mother is easily giving, and mothers, too, are entitled to their preferences and may be more giving with one child than another.

Sometimes the "ungivingness" may simply be a characteristic of the mother and may not at all indicate that she doesn't love her child. It may only mean that she inhibits the expression of affection, that she is an undemonstrative person. Usually, this comes about when the mother, herself, was brought up to feel that her emotions were not valuable. Perhaps her parents were incapable of dealing with much emotion. She may even have been punished by disapproval or by being humiliated for showing her feelings. As one woman said, "To show my parents my feelings was like telling them the vulnerable places they could hurt me, and they did. So I put my feelings in a cold, steel vault. And I still rarely take them out." She even had trouble hugging her own children and could tolerate their sitting on her lap for only brief minutes when they were small. She cared very deeply about her children, but when they were small, they would complain that she wouldn't sit with them for a few minutes when she put them to bed, and now, as adults, they often accuse her of coldness.

But it may not be only that you are unexpressive of your

feelings. If your child is saying that you don't love him, it may mean that, despite the great myth that all mothers love their children, the truth could be that you don't really love your child. That possibility, that you don't love your child, is perhaps one of the most difficult for any mother even to contemplate. It is a taboo thought, a forbidden idea. It is assumed that maternal love instinctively comes with motherhood, and that a mother who doesn't love her child is an unnatural mother. But it does *not* come instinctively, and many mothers, if they dared to be honest, would admit that they don't really love their grown-up offspring —and maybe never did.

What would keep a mother from loving her adult son or daughter? The most obvious place to look first is at the characteristics of that child and how he is with his mother. Did the child develop in ways that turned off her loving feelings? One mother said, "I know I loved her so much when she was little, and I enjoyed her growing. I have no doubts about it. I was crazy about her. But she began to change in ways I couldn't take. You probably think I mean that she grew up differently from my expectations, and I couldn't take not being in control. But it isn't that. She got in with people whose ways I find abhorrent, and she became a person I wouldn't have anything to do with if she were someone else's child. She's totally self-centered, and in her relationship with me, she was persistently mean and unpleasant. I'm sure I had something to do with it all; I even think I understand what, but it doesn't make me like her. And now, I think I've stopped loving her. That's supposed to be terrible, isn't it? But it's true. I love who she once was, but I can't kid myself into thinking I love her now."

There can often be this sad progression, from a mother uttering those trite but often true words, "I love you but I don't like what you're doing," to feeling, "I love you but I don't like you," and finally to feelings of dislike and unlove.

Apart from the type of person that specific grown-up child is, there are many possible reasons why a mother may not love her child. Perhaps the child came into her life at the wrong time, from the viewpoint of her feeling ready, or of her feelings toward her husband, or her feeling the child as interfering with other aspects of her life, or of her capacity to cope with the parental job. Perhaps she never wanted that job but felt channeled by social pressures, or coerced by her husband or her parents to go against her own preferences and needs. Perhaps her child reminded her of someone else whom she didn't like—her mother or father, her Aunt Minny, her husband or herself. And perhaps the child himself was not very lovable. From the very first, he may have been a child of difficult temperament.

But probably the most frequent reason for a mother's not loving her child is that the mother's inner child is operating too strongly. If the mother's personality is dominated largely by an inner child who is (as all small children are) self-centered, needing lots of applause and not wanting to take care of others' needs at the expense of putting off the gratification of her own needs, then she will be limited in her ability to love. She may be able to respond lovingly to her offspring when he is being just the way she wants him to be. But when her son or daughter has needs or wishes different from those she would prefer, or inconvenient to her, she will find it difficult to be loving.

While it is not easy to see yourself as a mother whose ability to love her children is limited, it is not impossible to see it if you examine your feelings with honesty. And it will help if you can accept that you are not a bad person, and you are not a failure as a woman if you have not been as loving as you would have wished to be with your child. Acknowledging this can be useful in several ways. You can then focus on the reasons for these restrictions on your lovingness. How did it come about? What were your parents like on this dimension? Were they loving or distant? Sensitive to you or self-preoccupied? Was there a loving facade over an underlying coldness? Were they so involved in you that you became self-centered in ways that limit your lovingness? And there are other difficult questions to face. Did I really want this child? Why? Or why not? Because I was afraid not to have one? Because what else does one do? Or because I really wished to grow and fulfill one aspect of myself by bringing forth and nurturing another being?

And was he the baby and child I really wanted? Was he the right sex? Did I like him? Does he remind me of someone else, or do I see him clearly as he is? Did I love him more once?

And above all you must ask yourself, Is my inner child demanding that my grown-up child be the way I want him to be as the price of my loving?

Why should you face such painful questions? For one thing, you may discover, after honest soul-searching, that you have *not* been particularly defective in your ability to love, but that this is largely a false charge arising out of the little child in your offspring who will accuse you of not loving him if you don't meet his every wish and expectation. If you conclude that this is the case, you are less likely to wilt with guilt at the charge, or to be defensive, or to counterattack, but you can turn your attention to dealing helpfully with that needy and demanding child within your son or daughter while at the same time holding your ground as a parent who is offering an adult-to-adult relationship. For example, if your child is accusing you of not loving him because you refused to give or lend him money for a purpose important to him, and you are convinced that your decision had nothing to do with a limitation of your lovingness but was a judgment you arrived at by looking at the total picture, you would be able to say, "I can see that you'd feel terribly disappointed and might believe I don't care about you, but I'm sure that's not true. These are my reasons for saying no. . . . Perhaps I can help you figure out other ways to accomplish what you want."

But even if your agonizing self-appraisal leads to finding that you have had difficulties in being loving, there are many good reasons to face these questions and their uncomfortable answers squarely. First, not facing them may have contributed to whatever trouble you are having with your child now.

Second, if you don't recognize the "unloving mother" part of you, you will be acting to conceal it in ways that make your relationship with your child feel phony to you both.

Third, as you acknowledge and understand the roots of your unloving feelings, you may be able to forgive yourself for not being the ideal mother you wished to be.

Fourth, in acknowledging and accepting your limitations as a reality, you will be less subject to emotional blackmail from your offspring, based on his terrible accusations that you don't love him. These accusations may lose some of their force to provoke guilt after you've come to terms with what your feelings are.

Fifth, you can deal with it in a straightforward way with your child, taking a stance that says, "I know I have limitations and I'm sorry, but I can only be who I am. I may try to give you more, but it may not work, and you and I may have to accept that 'That's all there is, there isn't anymore.' And then perhaps we can both relax and see what relationship is now possible."

Finally the self-acknowledgement, self-acceptance and new authenticity in relating to your son or daughter may in itself increase your ability to love him and may make him respond in ways that are more lovable.

Mother and Daughter

Some of the specific sources of anger you find directed at you can differ, depending on whether your angry child is a son or daughter. And one of the most frequent accusations of daughters these days, although often not directly stated to their mothers, is that mother failed to prepare them for effective *independent* living. They complain that she did not teach them self-reliance, nor did she provide, by example, a model of female self-sufficiency. A young woman who consulted me was having much difficulty advancing in the business world to which she had returned after her children were in their adolescence. Despite obvious intelligence and talent, she would not do the right thing at the right time to further her career. She became aware of an underlying rage toward her parents, particularly her mother, for not giving her the attitudes and motivation she needed for this kind of pursuit. To help her clarify her jumbled feelings about this, I suggested she write a "letter" (never to be sent) to them expressing this anger. Here are excerpts from her writing.

Dear Mother and Father,

How little the world likes its women out of place. In this you were absolutely right. A happy woman is one who knows her place. You must have thought a woman who knew her place liked that place. Alas, you raised a daughter who didn't. From the beginning I didn't and I am mad at you, angry, furious, outraged, in fact, that you ignored me. You did. Why didn't you buy me a chemistry set? Who

> bought me those goddamn dolls and the baby carriage when it was clear I didn't want them? . . . Striving was not in your vocabulary for me except for a husband. I hate you for giving me a single life goal—*a husband!* What a useless, dependent, parasitic, futile, self-defeating goal for anyone! Would you teach your son to grow up desiring only to have a wife? . . . I love your alternatives. If no husband, then teaching. Elementary teaching. Bookkeeping. There were two careers in the whole wide world for women: bookkeeping and teaching. And wiving and mothering. And growing prosperous, and taking care of parents as they grow older, and giving parties on the right occasions. Terrific goals. . . . Oh, Mother, what a job you did on me!

If her mother is holding her too closely (You Bother Me Too Much), a daughter will not only chafe at the feeling of being held on a leash, but will see her mother's need for close involvement as a manipulation of her insecurity and dependence. One woman in her early thirties told me, "I despise my mother and have despised her almost for as long as I can remember. I didn't know why I had that feeling as a child, because she was always there for me, taking care of me. . . . When I was in my early teens, a group of us wanted to sleep out in a tent in the backyard of my friend's house, right down the block. The other girls got permission, but my mother said no. When I told my friends, one of them said, 'Your mother is always so overprotective.' I had never heard the term before, but it fit, and I felt so ashamed of myself and angry with my mother. . . . Years later I realized that was only part of the reason for my anger. The main reason was that she was so tied to me and my sister that I felt there was no real person there. I felt so passive and weak because she was my model of womanhood. Fortunately, I saw other women who were different. But I still get furious when my mother pulls the 'How come I never hear from you? bit with that lost hurt tone in her voice. I feel like saying, 'Dammit, don't you have a life of your own?' "

This kind of feeling among young adult women has been intensified by the societal developments of the last few decades that now beckon women with more options as to how they may live fulfilling lives. This has deepened the feelings of dislike and resentment many adult daughters feel toward mothers whom they see as having lived constricted and dependent lives. What is a mother to do when confronted with such a serious charge? A lot will depend on how she evaluates the basis for her daughter's anger. If it is your daughter who is making the accusation, ask yourself two questions. First, Do I feel that my way of life as a woman really reflects a fear, a weakness, a lack of independence? And second, Does my wish to be as close as I'd like to be with her mean I don't have enough of a separate life of my own?

If your answer to these questions is yes, then you will have to decide what, if anything, you would like to do about living in a position where you feel weak and less than a full person and from which your inner child leans on your daughter for maintaining a feeling of comfortable attachment and belonging. You don't have to do anything, but if you don't, you run the risk that your daughter's anger will remain and be an ever present barrier between you.

Suppose your answer to these questions is no, or largely no. Then it is necessary to state where you are in very clear terms. "Look, according to how I was brought up and what I believe, my role of being the homemaker, of seeing to Dad's needs and the children's needs is not a weakness but a considerable strength. It does not make me less of a person, but more of a person. The world has changed, and there are new roles in which women are finding their strength, and I have not been a good model of that for you. Sorry. But I'm not going to let you make me feel like something powerless and parasitic just because there are changes in what women can do. I won't criticize or demean your choice of the path that makes sense for you, and I don't want you putting me down for choosing my way. As for wanting closeness to you, perhaps in part it does come from some little girl need in me to feel attached, but mostly it comes out of a very natural wish to have continuity with my own daughter. Unless you can see that, you will only resent me. Trust that I have no wish to smother you, and have faith that you are too strong to let me if I did want to. I don't want a relationship in which I feel you are contemptuous of who I am or in which you defend yourself against me."

Conveying that you feel strong within your role and that you are independent enough not to want a relationship with her if it reeks of her disdain, if put forth consistently in your actions as well as your words, will probably permit your daughter to respond to you with a fresh step instead of the old Song and Dance.

Mothers and Sons

Mothers who have tended to hold on to sons too long and too tightly are often attacked not only for being controlling and smothering (You Bother Me Too Much), but for being castrating. The son may not use that word, but he will feel and express that his mother's need to keep him close takes something away not only from his independence, but from his manhood. "I don't care if the girls call you every day," a young married man screamed at his mother, "I'm not one of the girls! I'm a man with a wife of my own and important responsibilities. What do you want me to do, call more often to discuss how to make chicken fricassee?"

The inner child of this son carried around the emotional memories of the many times he felt put down by his mother's controlling role in his early life. That little boy has been so humiliated and angered by his mother's need to hold on that he has lost all ability to differentiate when she was too controlling and when she was offering appropriate parental limits and supervision. That little boy cannot differentiate whether the controlling measures of his mother were based on her need to keep him dependent on her, or because he was her child, or because he was a male. And that inner little boy does not allow this son, now grown, to see that some of her requests may not come from needs to hold on to him or emasculate him, but may arise from her own little girl anxieties and/or her own maternal caring.

Confronted with his attack, this mother was confused and felt misunderstood. "I'm not telling him he's not a man just because I ask him how he is." But perhaps the needs of her inner child for closeness blinded her to her son's needs for greater recognition of his independence and his manhood and prevented her from seeing the infuriating impact she was having on him.

When a son feels that his mother has been too distant and separate, not only will he blame her for depriving him of closeness (You Don't Love Me), but he may feel that she did not love him *because he was a male*, or *as a male*, and that she cheated him of the self-confidence that comes with the feeling that a woman can adore him. "Now I've found someone who really loves me as her man, and it makes me aware that there wasn't anything wrong with me—it was just that you didn't or couldn't love me." And his mother responded with all sincerity, "I loved you more than I ever loved anyone. I'm just not very demonstrative." This angry Song and Dance is between a little girl, whose fear of the vulnerability of closeness, particularly with a male (this mother's own father died when she was seven, a terribly painful loss), has caused her to constrict her ability to express her tender feelings, and a little boy who could not help but take her reticence as a personal rejection. Grown-ups they may now be, but neither can find a way out of the hostilities that were engendered by this child-to-child interaction.

I cannot stress too strongly that if you, as a mother, are being accused by your son of being too controlling, then he is experiencing it not only as a smothering, not only as treating him like a baby, but as a belittlement of his manliness. You may do this unintentionally, particularly in those early adult years as your son goes from late adolescence into his early twenties. Your perceptions of him may lag behind, still seeing him as a little boy, perhaps still wanting him to be a little boy, and with your words or actions, you may become quite "matronizing." And the resentments engendered then (or that exacerbate even earlier feelings) can last a long time unless you take corrective steps. As always, the first step is the recognition of what is happening. The mother of a twenty-year-old boy said, "Once he was complaining to me that I was being bitchy—it was some little mother-son battle, I can't even remember about what—but I realized I was being controlling and he was right. I had to make a conscious decision that if I wanted to maintain a relationship with this son of mine, I had to recognize he was a separate person who thinks differently from me about some things, and if I kept it up I'd alienate him. I became aware that I had to move away, give him his own space, that he was now a man who had a right to make his own decisions. Since then it feels different, very nice. I can stand back and see him more as a person—and I can be less involved with things about him I don't like."

It is that moment of recognition of your child's separateness and adulthood that, for your son, is an affirmation not only of his "grown-upness," but his manliness. He may not be able to respond to it all at once. You are the one he has known primarily from the position of a little boy, and he will still tend to be wary of you and his own secret wishes to continue to be your little boy. But if you maintain a clear view of his manhood, he is more likely to open himself to a new and less hostile response.

A Separate Peace

You may be puzzled and discouraged at how tenacious your child's anger is, how unyielding it is to efforts to reason, to talk it out or to offer the olive branch. *You have to consider the possibility that your son or daughter is holding on to his anger as a way of holding on to you.*

That may feel like a strange thought. Anger as a way of holding on to you. You have experienced your child's anger as an attack designed to hurt you and push you away, not draw you closer. But anger, intense and ever present, can be like a thick, braided cable of highly charged wires that bind you and your child together with an electric intensity. Anger is not an absence of feeling. It is not a space. It is not indifference. It is a powerful and stimulating emotion. It is involvement. Is the man I know who, angry at his mother, sent her a lemon on Mother's Day less involved than someone who sent a bouquet of flowers?

So your son's or daughter's anger at you is a deep connection. Mostly it comes from the little boy or girl in him who is still trying to resolve the dependence-independence conflict, still telling you that you're smothering him or don't care about him. This does not mean you have nothing at all to do with his anger. You may be too intrusive; you may be too distant; you may be using old techniques of being a martyr who provokes guilt, or a controller who has to have her say and her way, or a saint who tells him what's right and what's wrong. Or a user of any dozens of techniques that could drive anyone up the wall and into a rage.* But

* More about these techniques and the Songs and Dances they are part of in Chapters 2 and 6.

it might help the child within you, whose fear of losing your son or daughter may be the driving force behind your maneuvers, to know that your offspring's anger is an expression of a bond rather than an abandonment.

But it is not a good bond. It is destructive of good feelings, destructive of peace of mind. It is a drainer of energy and can cause wear and tear on your body. This is particularly so if the child in you engages in an angry battle with the angry child in your son or daughter. Sure, you'll be deeply involved with each other, but at what cost?

So, noting that his or her anger reflects a wish *not* to terminate a tie with you, perhaps you can relax enough to back off, to tell the child in you that she is not being abandoned, and to allow the mature parenting part to take over. If you can keep yourself from responding as that little girl inside yourself, you are on your way to ending the old frustrating Song and Dance based on harsh words, discordant music, jarring tempo. In *Fear of Flying,* Isabella Wing says of her sister, "Randy blamed my mother for everything: from not changing her diaper often enough to changing it too often; from giving her piano lessons too young to not letting her go skiing young enough."* If you are the mother of a Randy, it would be so tempting to defend heatedly the pacing of Randy's piano lessons, skiing lessons, and diaper changes. Or you could easily go on the offensive and call her crazy, a liar, or an ingrate.

But suppose you see that the little girl inside grown-up Randy is caught in the unresolved issue of symbiosis and separateness, swinging from indicting you for holding her too close to blaming you for pushing her toward independence. And then suppose you don't respond from your inner child but instead take the position, "I did it the way I did it, and I'm truly sorry if it was wrong for you, but that's in the unchangeable past. I know that I love you and want us to get along. If you can let go of the old angers, maybe we can find a way to have a relationship we will both enjoy."

In doing this, you will have stopped your part in the Song and Dance. That's half the battle. Your son or daughter may keep

* Erica Jong, *Fear of Flying*, p. 258.

dancing solo, maybe for a while, maybe forever. The chances are he'll soon notice he's dancing alone, and perhaps after some frenzied efforts to invite you or incite you back onto the dance floor, he, too, may put down the anger. But whether he does or not, the fact that you refused to join him in it is a great and liberating victory in itself.

CHAPTER 4

High Noon

"I don't understand it, and I've tried. We were really pals when Mike was a kid, and now we're barely speaking. He has so much anger that anything I do makes it worse. It's really like a state of war."

There was bitterness apparent in the voice as well as the words of this father. And I have heard that same bitter tone from other fathers who find themselves in an unwanted war with their sons or daughters. I have heard it with enough frequency to make me wonder if there is something in the very nature of a father-child relationship that makes it particularly vulnerable to a dramatic deterioration from caring to hostility.

To explore this question, we must first ask what the role of a father is all about. To a great extent, the role of the father is the same as the mother's. He too should be close and nurturing when the child is very small, and then, in accordance with the child's developing capacities, he must encourage greater independence. But the father also has another crucial function. The child has emerged from mother's body. As an infant, he may have been nourished at her breasts. Probably this young child has spent more time with mother than with father and has had more of his physical and emotional needs met by mother than by father. Therefore, the tendency to maintain the old fusion with his mother can be considerably stronger and run much deeper than similar inclinations with his father. The child also has innate strivings to develop all those burgeoning potentials that will make him strong and autonomous. As we have seen, the mature parenting part of the mother will want to aid and abet these strivings. "But both mother and child often need help, the mother because she may have deep needs of her own to hold on to the child, the child because separation is always beset with anxiety. And here it is the father who must take the child by the hand and stroll with him into the larger world, showing him its joys and bedazzlement, teaching him to deal with its dangers, imparting to him the courage and confidence to be out there. At his best, the father is also available to the little child within the mother who may be upset and threatened during this time of separation. *The essential job of the father, then, is to help the mother and child separate from each other.*"*

So the role of the father is very complex. Not only does he have to be aware of the child's changing needs of dependence and independence in relation to himself, but as the *other* parent, he must be sensitive to that primal attachment between his wife and his child and help each in the struggle to loosen the tie. When the child feels that his father has failed him in any aspect of this unacknowledged task, he is likely to be angry, and his father is likely to be confused and chagrined by that anger.

A Charlie Brown Father

For example, there's Mr. Barnes, the owner of a small furniture store, who was being honored with a special award from his lodge for years of dedicated service. He had called his daughter, Nancy, to invite her and her husband to the award dinner. She usually avoided seeing him, and this occasion was to be no exception. He told me he practically begged her to go and continued to badger her after her repeated refusals. Finally, she exploded and

* Howard Halpern, *Cutting Loose*, p. 58.

screamed at him, "They'll be honoring you for being some sort of super grand exalted potentate, and that will make me sick because I know what a weak nothing you really are."

Mr. Barnes was crushed and seething. "I worked long hours in the store just hanging in there in bad times so Nancy could have nice things, so she could have an education, so she could hold her head up. Is that being a weak nothing?"

I got to talk to Nancy about the incident, and she was feeling a little guilty about what she had said but had not changed her view of her father. "He was a hardworking provider, that's true. I rarely saw him, but that wouldn't make me feel the anger that I'm feeling now. I could understand that. It's the way he was with me and my mother when he *was* there. My mother is strong-willed, self-centered and domineering. That's not just my opinion. She knows what's best for everyone about everything. I felt overwhelmed by her, like a doll she would dress and wind up and send out to turn this way and that by her remote control. I longed to have my father stand up to her, but he was as controlled by her as I was. Maybe more so. I think he was terrified of her. . . .

"He seemed to have no preferences about anything—where we lived, where we vacationed, what we did on weekends. Nothing. He'd say, 'I don't care. Whatever you'd like.' I can't believe he really had no preferences. He was just afraid to disagree with her. A few times I saw him argue about something with her, but all she had to do was start yelling or crying, and he'd say 'Okay, okay take it easy. Have it your way. It's not important.' And sometimes it was terribly important, at least to me, because often it involved me. He backed down on buying me a bicycle because she said it would make *her* nervous. He backed down on supporting my wanting to take one of those cross-country teen bus tours when I was fourteen because she wanted me to go with her to this beach house we used to rent. And so many other things. . . . I remember a few times when he punished me because my mother pushed him to it. In fact, he'd even say afterward, 'Next time you'll listen to your mother.'

"And it's not all long-ago things. A couple of years ago, I was worried about something in my marriage, and for some reason I thought he'd be able to advise me. He was so uncomfortable. He said something about asking mother, and I screamed that it was his advice I wanted. He said things that were so wishy-washy, like always. Charlie Brown may be a nice guy, but do you know what it's like to have him for a father?''

So Nancy is enraged at her father for failing her in that essential fathering job of helping her to become separate from her mother, of being that "other" parent who gives her the support and strength to deal with the larger world. Mr. Barnes cannot understand this because he knows that he has been well intentioned, cared deeply, and done his best. "Sure I go along with my wife a lot, but she's a very nervous woman. Often I purposely avoided making waves for Nancy's sake. It's not good for a child to be brought up with yelling—to see her parents fight."

Mr. Barnes loved Nancy very much. He wanted to know what he could do to improve the relationship. He recognized that he would have to look more deeply into both Nancy and himself. He began to see Nancy's struggle as a little girl to become a person separate from her overbearing mother and how much Nancy needed his help in the struggle and noted the ways he did come through and the ways he didn't. And he recognized that the struggle is never finished for anyone, that it still goes on in Nancy, and that the little girl in Nancy still feels she needs him to be a strong support on the side of her wish to be independent as against her tendency to retreat to safe dependence.

Further, Mr. Barnes saw that he would have to face many questions. To what extent was his subservience to his wife really to foster a more harmonious home for Nancy, and to what extent did it come from his own little boy fears of his wife's disapproval? To the child in himself, does his wife stand for his own mother? If so, does that make her love and approval so desperately crucial that he continues to surrender many of his desires and much of his potency in order to avoid her wrath and prevent the withdrawal of her love? Is this why he let Nancy down? Is this why she is so angry?

Mr. Barnes had the considerable courage it takes to face these questions. He admitted that he had no strong drive to make any major changes in his personality or in the basic nature of his relationship with his wife. But he decided to make one change in his relationship with Nancy. Instead of quickly putting his wife on the phone every time Nancy called, he got into conversations with her. And he sometimes called Nancy from his store to see how she was doing and to chat. This was new. He had never permitted himself much of a separate relationship with her. Nancy responded with puzzled reluctance at first, then seemed to appreciate and enjoy his calls. Occasionally, he invited Nancy to have lunch with him. Mrs. Barnes seemed uneasy about this turn of events, but it was clear her husband was not asking her permission. At one of their lunchtime get-togethers, Mr. Barnes told Nancy, "You know, I understand I didn't help you out much in standing up to Mom, and that wasn't right. But Nan, it also wasn't right for you to see only that and not to see that I did a lot of good things, too." Nancy could recognize her father's new steps in developing a relationship with her apart from her mother and the strength that took, and this enabled her to let her father's words in. The anger between them was getting defused, and they began to enjoy a newfound relationship.

"I Don't Sleep Well"

In his quest to become a free-standing individual, the child may be angry not only at a father who was too wishy-washy, absent or "underwhelming" to help him in this effort, but at a father who was so authoritarian or even despotic that the child felt squelched or put down. Instead of feeling father as a support of his drive to become strong and independent, he felt father as the enemy of that drive, as someone who undermined his self-confidence and kept him weak and dependent. This change is particularly difficult for a father to understand because, as far as he can see, he always meant to help and strengthen his child by giving him some of his own strength through his advice and direction.

An example of this is the father who, in the opening paragraph of this chapter, spoke of his relationship with his son as "like a state of war." He was perplexed and deeply wounded by Mike's intense and unremitting anger. He tried to make sense of it.

"I was a busy man when Mike was growing up, trying to establish myself, but I always tried to have time for him. We would take him everywhere with us when he was small. Later, he didn't like that and often preferred being with his friends, but that was normal. During the summers, starting when he was about fifteen, he worked for me at my office. I would treat him like any other employee, but we'd drive to and from work together, and we'd talk about things, and I'd tell him about the business. I put him through an Ivy League college, and then he wanted to go to law school, which was fine with me, and I put him through that. I was proud of him. I financed his first office and got him some clients.

"I noticed Mike was getting distant and a little touchy. Sometimes I thought he was avoiding his mother and me. Then, Mike got married. I thought she was a lovely girl, but after his marriage he began to get really hostile for no reason. I think she turned him against us. We'd ask them to come over on a Sunday, and he didn't just politely refuse, but there'd be a silence and then a cold, 'No, we're busy.' If I pushed our getting together, or even tried for more frequent phone calls, he would get furious. His mother was particularly upset, so I went down to his office to have a talk with him. I told him what I'm telling you now. He blew up, accused me of always trying to control his life. . . . I tried to reason with him and tell him I didn't want to own him but just to be close like a family should, but he kept digging up things from the past, things I don't even remember. I was amazed. The look on his face was beyond anger. It was hate. I blew up and said lots of things I guess I shouldn't have, but he was so arrogant, accusing. He threw me out of his office. He just kept saying, 'Get out. I don't want you here.' I was being thrown out of the office I had bought every stick of furniture for, every file cabinet. . . . I felt humiliated when I walked past his secretary who I'm sure heard everything.

"Since then—two years—the war is always there, even when we're being civil. And sometimes, on those rare occasions when we visit, we begin fighting all over again. I used to think we'd always be buddies, we'd be a family. I even used to dream about our being business partners some day. Sure, I'm sad about it, and I'm angry at the betrayal of me and his mother and our hopes. To tell you the truth, I don't sleep well since all this."

When I spoke to Mike he said, "Look, I'm as close to them as I want to be. I have nothing to say to my mother. She's always had a way of making me feel like I'm letting her down without saying a word. I could bear that because I do love her a lot, but my father is impossible. He is so arrogant and bossy, and he doesn't even know it. He always tried to control my life. When I was younger I liked it because he helped coach our neighborhood baseball team when it was hard to get other fathers to take an interest. But whenever I wanted to go in my own direction or have an idea he didn't like, he'd cut me down.

"You say he told you of the car rides those summers I worked for him. He often brings that up. They were mostly torture for me. He would tell me about the business, and at first I felt so grown-up that he shared those mysterious terms with me like 'equity' and 'customer's man' and 'accounts receivable.' They seemed like passwords into the world of adult men. But as soon as I told him some of my ideas to improve the business he'd snort, actually snort, and make fun of it. There was never even, 'That's an interesting idea but there are some drawbacks,' just sarcasm and dismissal. I began to clam up on those trips and not talk. Once I purposely counted that we drove there and back a total of thirty-one times without my saying a word, and he never noticed. The only reason I said anything the thirty-second time was that my father interrupted his monologue to say, 'You seem awfully quiet today.'

"The feeling that he owned me got worse when he paid for my college and law school. And I should never have let him finance my office, but I was broke and in the habit of his taking care of things. My office is in the building *he* thought I should be in. When he tried to get Betty and me to buy a house where *he* thought we should live, and held tempting carrots under our noses to move us in that direction, and ridiculed our taste and judgment about where *we* wanted to live, and how we lived, and just insisted on treating us like recalcitrant children, I began to get furious and tried to pull back from him. But he's used to getting his way, so he came on stronger, and I've had to tell him where to go. I can't stand being in the same room with him now. I find my whole body clenches up."

Mike has reasons for his anger. His father has reasons to feel hurt and betrayed. After all, hadn't he done the fatherly job of taking Mike by the hand to "stroll with him into the large world, showing him its joys and bedazzlement, teaching him to deal with its dangers, imparting to him the courage and confidence to be out there''? He coached Mike's baseball team, he taught him about the business world, he sent him to a fine college and law school, and he helped him set up in practice. If that isn't launching a child properly to be on his own, then what is? And yet Mike treats him like an enemy. Mike has experienced his father differently. He feels that his father, instead of facilitating his development and supporting his autonomy was controlling and directing him, was launching him not to find his own trajectory, but to be a satellite revolving around his dad in a preset orbit.

In some ways, Mike's father did help him to separate from his mother. He was a model for being freewheeling, assertive, and for making it out there in the world away from the hearth. But his need to be the boss with everyone, including his own son, could only strip Mike of self-confidence, not build it. When Mike began to gain his self-confidence, he turned on his father with the same aggressiveness for which his father had been the model.

Am I a ''Despotic Dad''?

If we were to look at the inner child of Mike's father, we would catch a glimpse of what the inner child of a domineering father is often like—an insecure little boy who is covering up his insecurities with bravado, with control and with commands that say, ''I'm the big man around here. Do it my way or else.''

If you are being accused of being such a despotic dad, you've got some very potent questions to ask yourself. Am I really like that? Why? Is it coming from the mature parent part of me? Or, honestly, am I a spoiled brat who must have his own way? If I am, how did I get that way? Do I really feel that powerful or is it a cover-up for feelings of weakness? For fear that unless I had control over people, including my children, they would not pay attention to me? That nobody would care about me if I didn't own them? That the world is a shaky place if I am not directing it? And if I am being domineering, what impact is this having on my children? Is it part of why my son or daughter is so angry at me? If it is and I want to improve the relationship, do I dare back off and let my children be separate and powerful in their own right?

Because that's just what it will need—the recognition that your children are separate and powerful in their own right, that they are in no way your possessions, and that they will usually know what's best for them better than you do. So you will have to stop trying to tell them what to do, either directly or indirectly. You will have to stop all belittlement of them and their decisions. If you care to give them anything, there will have to be no strings attached (such as financing Mike's office and then directing him as to where it should be located).

In other words, it will mean *respecting* your children. And in respecting them, you will be giving yourself, at the same moment, the gift of feeling pride in the job you did in bringing them to independent adulthood. And it will mean taking the risk of laying down your sceptre and daring to discover whether they will still love you enough and respect you enough not to thumb their nose or disappear.

It will take a lot of courage to do that. Because the fact of the matter is, if enough angry rebelliousness has accumulated in your children, they may well choose to thumb their nose and disappear. After all, they can't be expected instantly to accept a change in you after all these years. But if it's genuine, if it comes through that you really respect them as separate and equal, the lifetime reservoir of powerful shared experiences of all kinds should afford a basis for a renewed relationship.

What if My Child Is Wrong to Be Angry?

Whether the charge against you was that you were too weak or too distant to help them separate from their mother and deal with the world, or too supervisory and overpowering to enable them to develop their own capacities, their accusations may not be correct. Your offspring's inner child can distort your behavior just as your inner child can distort his.

For example, your children may indict you for having been too weak to support them with mother or school or the world, but what may be going on is that the child in them wants you always to be on their side, always to agree with them, to make things easy for them. Very small children make this demand and your grown-up offspring may be expressing that long-ago feeling. Their anger may be a childish tantrum at not getting their way or at being forced to deal with troublesome or arduous situations on their own instead of having you take care of such situations for them. And very small children want their parents to be perfect and powerful. They especially want their father to be Superman. The child inside your grown-up son or daughter may still be enraged at you for having human failings and may be lashing out at you for them.

Or suppose the indictment is that you have been too tyrannical and bossy. Coming from the child within them, this could mean that you held high standards and demanded that they be responsible and grown-up. Their anger, therefore, may be a childish tantrum for your not letting them get away with whatever they wanted to get away with. How do you know if you are dealing with a valid accusation or a distortion arising from their inner child?

There will probably always be some hint of truth to the accusations. People rarely spin such charges out of undyed wool. But the point is not whether you *were* tyrannical or simply firm, or whether you *were* insufficiently caring or simply an unexpressive person. What matters now is whether *today,* when they are adults, you are behaving the way their indictment reads. For example, if you were a despotic dad when they were young (and if you were, it would be helpful to acknowledge it to yourself and to them), your son or daughter, spurred and shaped by the stored anger from the past, may continue to paint you as a dictator long after you stopped being coercive with them. But if you have stopped acting like you own them, you would be in a position to say, "Look, I know I'm not doing that now. I've stopped being your supervisor, but you often act as if I'm still bossing you if I just state an opinion. If you persist on seeing me the old way, we can't get along."

It may take a long time for your offspring to discard his view of you from many years ago, but the more you dissociate yourself from it in your present behavior, by giving up the authoritarian role, the weak role, the indifferent role, or any other provoking position that may be arising from the child inside you, and the more you pursue a respectful man-to-man or man-to-woman relationship with them, the better they will be able to differentiate their child view of you from their current reality. Of course, if there is no change in you, if you still act like either a superior or a shadow with them, then their anger will continue and will probably get increasingly nasty.

Angry Daughters, Angry Sons

We have seen that the times we live in have led to specific charges that daughters will make against their mothers. The same is true about charges daughters may make, often with great bitterness, against their fathers. Fathers are of and in the world of man. Women are increasingly entering that once alien world, and some find that they are ill prepared for it, even lost in it. Naturally, they blame the person in their life who, being from that world, could have readied them to function more effectively out there. Why didn't you teach me what it was all about? Why didn't you encourage me to think of making it out there as an independent person? Why did you act disdainful or patronizing about my ambitions? Did you want just to pass me from your care to the care of another man like I was a pet cat or a brood mare? Why didn't you tell me about your work, or how to succeed, or what you have to know, and even the dirty games you have to play? You always assumed that my brother would have to know these things, and your expectations that he would someday function independently were there in the way you treated him from the time he was small. Why not me?

And they were often right; many fathers have not held a view of their daughters as persons who could or *should* become independent, successful individuals. But the world has changed, and if you have had these attitudes, your daughters have grounds for accusing you of selling them short. Yet, can you be blamed? You were a product of your own time, when daughters weren't thought of that way. But now when you know that women want to have the skills and attitudes that would permit independent functioning, and your daughter is angry at you for not imparting these to her, you can no longer plead ignorance. If you still hold these attitudes, then your daughter is likely to remain angry at you. If you don't, you will have to find ways to express this change in you. And most of all, you will have to be careful not to continue to express these attitudes out of habit. I recall a woman I know who told me in anger, "My brother just got his own office at the investment company he works for, and my father bought him a big and expensive oil painting to hang over his desk. I got my office as a senior editor for a big publishing house two years ago, and my father said, 'That's very nice,' but he never even gave me an ashtray." What had happened here? This father loved both his children but did not take his daughter's work or success as seriously as his son's. And his daughter was not about to forgive him for this.

From their early childhood, sons, too, know that their fathers live in that mysterious men's preserve, but they count on their fathers to help initiate them into it. Note how Mike spoke of learning the terms of business from his father, as if they were passwords into the world of men. When sons feel that their fathers have failed them by being weak or unavailable, they will be angry that father let them down in not sufficiently imparting to them or infusing them with the stuff of masculinity and the wherewithal to succeed. This can be surprisingly intense when they see their fathers as having erected a facade of power and success, but in the crunch or the long run prove to be ineffectual. The son will feel betrayed and furious at his father for being pompous and false. In *Death of a Salesman,* Willy Loman is always talking about how "well liked" he is, how his son Biff is also "well liked," and he holds this up as a sure key to success, if not tantamount to the success itself. Willy could not deal effectively with reality and he filled Biff with so many false feelings of greatness that Biff could not handle the mundane tasks needed to succeed. Finally Biff explodes at Willy, exposing the phoniness of it all and screaming, "And I never got anywhere because you blew me so full of hot air I could never stand taking orders from anybody." *

Like Mike, when a son feels that his father dominated him, he will wonder, as did one young man whose father would not let him make any independent decisions in the family business, Did my father lord it over me to teach me or because he saw me as a

* Arthur Miller, *Death of a Salesman* (New York: Viking, 1958).

rival he had to keep in check? His feeling that his father needed to hold him down fueled continuing anger.

Anger and the Family Song and Dance

If you can convert the situation from discord to harmony, the entire family would benefit, because the chances are the angry song and dance between you and your son or daughter has spread to every family member. This is particularly unavoidable if your child lives with you, where anger between any two members of the family can electrify the household. I interviewed a couple who spoke of what it was like when their son lived at home in a state of belligerence with his father. The wife talked of how uncomfortable the atmosphere was.

HUSBAND: I didn't have to *do* anything. Nor did I do anything. All we had to do was pass in the hallway, and I tell you that *sparks* literally jumped between us. He got the message. He got a very silent message. I don't think I ever said a word to him.

WIFE: They didn't talk at all; they didn't say one word to each other.

HUSBAND: Because I couldn't possibly have started to say anything and finish without at least 22,000 more words. . . .

WIFE: And I was finding it extremely unpleasant.

HUSBAND: But sparks literally *flew* when we passed one another —within two feet of one another.

WIFE: From four in the afternoon, I'd start thinking of inane things to say at the dinner table to try and make some connection. Because I couldn't stand nobody's talking to one another—three people sitting at the table and nobody saying a word. I would be talking. I'd ask a question and get a yes or no. I'd turn to the other and ask the same question and get a yes or no. But no conversation.

What an awful, brooding atmosphere in the place that is supposed to be one's harbor, one's source of replenishment and peace. And while such a situation can improve when the child no longer lives with the parents, a Song and Dance can swirl everyone into it, even when the family members live apart. We saw how Mike had much less contact with his mother than he would have if he weren't in an ongoing battle with his father. Mike's wife strongly sided with Mike and held many of Mike's attitudes toward his father, treating him courteously but with pointed distance. She was often in the position of turning down social invitations from Mike's mother, thus putting these two women in uncomfortable conflict. And the tendency for Mike and his wife to spend more time with his wife's parents caused hostility between the two parental families. If Mike and his wife are to go on and have children, it is not difficult to see that these youngsters would soon soak up the family tensions and might side with their parents against grandpa or feel guilty about how much they love and enjoy grandpa.

There is a great deal at stake for you to try to understand the conflict between your child and yourself, to see if the little boy within you is involved in a Song and Dance with the little boy in your grown-up son or the little girl in your grown-up daughter, and to try to stop your end of it. "Why me?" you may ask. "Why don't you tell them to change what they're doing, to stop being so hostile?"

It would be nice if your children were to change their contribution to the Song and Dance, but what if they don't? What if, at this point, they are not interested in changing it? Do you then just keep it going? That's one option, and lots of people take it, and the Song and Dance goes on to the grave. But if it is to change, and obviously you are interested in making changes or you wouldn't be reading this book, you will have to make some new moves. You know that you are hurting. You know you don't like it. And you've probably discovered by now that your old ways of dealing with the problem are not working. So, practically speaking, if the relationship is to improve, it has to start with you.

"But still," you may protest, "it's not fair that the burden is all on me. He is giving me a very hard time, is being downright nasty. Do I have to take that abuse and just search my soul?" *Emphatically not*. Being the initiator of steps to improve the situation does not mean passively surrendering to your child's angry assaults. In fact, nothing at all is likely to change unless and until you make it clear that you will not tolerate the continuation of their abuse. The abuse I am referring to is not the occasional furious outburst by your child; such explosions can occur in the normal course of any relationship. But when your offspring is chronically assailing and castigating you, you cannot allow it to continue. *Your first priority must be a refusal to become involved in any interaction with them in which you are being abused.*

If you so refuse, you will be preventing the continuation of a whole range of Songs and Dances: the stormy Songs and Dances in which you are angry and abusive in return; the simpering Songs and Dances in which you plead, almost on your knees, for their acceptance and approval; the intricate Songs and Dances in which you try to buy them, or manipulate them, or appease them; the arrogant Songs and Dances in which you try by command or threat to get them to respect you, or be with you, or be nice to you, or do what you say. Or any of a large number of Songs and Dances which have in common that the child in you, fearful of abandonment, uneasy at not having control, angry at not having his way, determines your response to your son or daughter. If you can stop responding from your inner child and respond as a self-respecting adult and mature parent who will not take this treatment from anyone, you could communicate, "Regardless of what anger you may hold, I am not here to be attacked, dumped on and treated badly. That must stop. Though I love you, I would rather have no contact with you at all than have you continue to abuse me. If you stop the persistent attacks, then maybe we can talk about how we can change things. But I will not listen to your needs or complaints while you are assaulting me with your words or actions."

This stance does not take the place of the need for you to evaluate the basis for your child's anger or to make changes in ways that you may be continuing to provoke that anger. But the maintenance of this stance, in ending the old Songs and Dances, makes it possible for a new and much more gratifying interaction to happen. This will not automatically dispel your son's or daughter's anger, but it can go a long way toward that if you maintain the two-branched position of refusing to be abused and trying to understand the basis of their anger and yours. Even if they should not immediately enter into a more satisfying relationship, you have gained much by ending your participation in an old pattern that was ineffectual, frustrating, and bad for your peace of being.

CHAPTER 5

As Long As He Needs Me

It didn't surprise me to hear many parents complain about not seeing their kids often enough, or not hearing from them enough, or generally feeling there was little connection between them and their grown-up children. What did surprise me was the very large number of parents who were concerned and uneasy that their adult sons or daughters were still too dependent on them, still insufficiently on their own two feet. Here are a few typical expressions of this worry.

> My son, Charles, is twenty-seven. We have two older children in their thirties who are married and have been out of the house for a long time, but Charles still lives with us. He's got a good job and makes enough to afford his own place. We want him to move out for his sake and ours. At his age he should be on his own, and at our age, so should we. But each time he's about ready to make the move, he goes into debt on some big purchase, like a new car or a trip to Europe. We don't know how strong a stand to take because it's his home too, isn't it?

> I felt the same sense of loss most mothers do when my daughter got married. I liked it that she would call every

day, or that she'd want me to go with her for furniture, or that she wanted my advice. But I had begun to get really involved in a new job, and after a while I noticed that I was annoyed at her frequent calls and requests. Then my annoyance turned into concern because she seemed to *need* to have that much contact with me. Even being married she is still holding on to my apron strings.

My son starts out on a job, moves out, takes his own place, and then a few months later loses his job and can't afford to live away, so he plops back in on us. And if I complain, he says I don't care about him.

My daughter had been married six years when her marriage fell apart, and so did she. She moved into an apartment in our building and either spends most of her time with us or drops her son off so she can have "relief." I love my daughter and my grandson, but this is becoming a way of life. I've done that bit.

My son got married a few years ago and now, through a combination of his not making much money but spending a lot, both of them are always asking us for loans or to pick up the tab for things like their daughter's day camp and orthodontia. First of all, we're not that rich. And second, I don't think it's good for a married man to be so dependent on his parents.

What has happened so that these young people, grown-up in years, are so ungrown-up in their ability to live more independent lives? We have seen that the universal struggle, which starts at birth, between the drive to leave the parental orbit and the wish to cling to the parents for nurturance and protection can continue through life. For some, the drive to move out into the world and to achieve a great deal of autonomy is the stronger force. For others, the need to cling is more powerful. What makes for this difference in development?

We have to look for the answer in the history of each individual child. Innate temperamental factors and the child's degree of health or disability can influence the tendency toward dependence. One mother, worried about her older son's tendency rarely to go out socially and to stay close to her said, "He was a very, very seriously ill child for many years with illnesses of various sorts—out of the frying pan into the fire—he moved from one illness to another, which restricted some of his activities. When he gets to know someone, he is very gregarious, very giving and very happy, but it's difficult for him to break new frontiers." This same woman said of her other son, "He was born independent and has been from the first moment." This reminded me of how Bill Cosby, the comedian, spoke of his two children. He said the first was angelic, let them sleep, and gave them the feeling that parenthood was a cinch and they were perfect parents. Then the second was born, emerging with a cigarette in one hand and a martini in the other, saying, "Things are going to be different around here now."

But apart from temperamental differences, the most important determinant of independence versus dependence is in the relationship between the child and the parents. If the parents appropriately and realistically support the child's movement toward separateness, then he is less likely to cling and avoid independence. There are two ways in which parents can impair their child's movement toward self-reliance. One, obviously, is if the parents, out of their own inner child fears of losing their offspring, hold on too tightly or too long. The other, less obvious but potentially as impairing, is if the parents, out of inner child reactions against closeness or responsibility, push the child toward separateness too early and beyond the pace of what the child's stage of development can handle, thus creating a reaction of fearful clinging. So the parent who stops his toddler from playing on the seesaw in the playground when he is willing and able to do so and the parent who pushes his toddler to play on the seesaw when he is *not* yet willing and able to do so can have the same effect of hobbling the movement toward autonomy.

Carry My Son

An old joke tells of the woman who steps out of her chauffeured limousine at a posh resort hotel and begins ordering the porters to hold this and take that. Then she says to one porter, "And you carry my son. He's in the back seat." The porter soon calls out,

"But ma'am, your son is about thirty years old. Doesn't he know how to walk?" The woman draws herself up imperiously and says, "Thank God, he never had to learn."

Clearly, our influence as parents in this area of dependence is not necessarily limited to the early history of our offspring. When our sons and daughters make that transition from child to adult, it inevitably means a decrease of our control and a completion of that separateness that the inner child in us can feel as abandonment. We will do different things, depending on how dominated we are by that anxiety-driven inner child. If we encourage our adolescent or young adult progeny to claim their privacy, get jobs, take on responsibilities, go to college away from home and develop skills, ideas and friends of their own, we will have a far different impact on our children's development than if we discourage these things. One mother said, "I guess it isn't fair for me to complain now about his being still too dependent on us when I always told him, 'Be careful, don't do this, don't do that, don't tire yourself, don't take chances, don't get involved.' "*

Often, the grown-up child's dependent actions reflect his ambivalence about becoming independent. I interviewed a group of women with adult children, and one woman was concerned that her twenty-six-year-old son seemed to lean on her too much. "He's too concerned with what I think about his actions. Matt will call to discuss his problems at work and how unhappy he is about certain situations. . . . " Another woman in the group interrupted to say, "The thing that isn't fair about your description is that you failed to say that Matt has 3,000 miles between himself and you. The way you tell it, you make it sound like he's calling from the next town. He's put this distance between you, and yet he holds on to closeness by calling and telling you things."

We can sense the conflict in Matt. He has moved far away in order to establish his independence, yet the child in him still needs to hold on. (The nature of his calls were not just for ordi-

* When children are young adults, the dependence is much more likely to be caused by the parent's holding the child back than his pushing the child out too fast, but even at this age, the parent who *coerces* rather than encourages his adolescent or youthful child to do social and occupational things for which he feels unready may end up with a young adult who, either symbolically or actually, resists leaving home.

nary continuation of contact and family feeling but came out of his neediness.) Perhaps his struggle has been sharpened by his mother's conflict. She said, "I'm ambivalent about his calling a lot because part of me likes his confiding in me, and part of me is unhappy that he isn't mastering the world."

The Sixties Generation

Parents who had children who were adolescents during the 1960s often faced, and may still be facing, very specific concerns that do not confront, to the same degree, those parents whose children traversed their adolescence before or since. To be an adolescent in the sixties was to be particularly vulnerable to the purported glories of drugs, to be part of a youth culture that was rebelliously anti-establishment, and to be part of a student body that valued anti-achievement. The best and the brightest were often swept into this counterculture tidal wave, and it made many of them more self-directed in their thinking and approach to their lives.

But it also had many damaging effects. Besides the fact that a few did not survive the effects of too much drug intake or too many bad trips, it often killed off motivation to develop some of their capacities for effective living. Youths caught up in resisting education, though seemingly out of motives of rebellious independence, often deprived themselves of the education and training and sense of responsibility that would have allowed them to build the muscles needed for real autonomy. Some of them developed these capacities later. Others, now in their thirties, still function like grown-up children, ineffectual and unable to sustain responsibility. Besides the fact that this rebellious youth culture often created antagonisms between parents and their offspring that, in some instances, have never been fully repaired, many of these young people who precipitously broke away during that period later came back, older yet even more dependent on their parents than before they left.

Aggressive Dependency

The dependent child is not always passive and clinging. At times, the dependency can be aggressive and demanding. Jody, for example, had been brought up in a large Tudor-style house in one of the East's wealthier suburbs. He was nineteen and in his second year at an Ivy League college when his parents came to consult me. His father was angry and belligerent. His mother sat quietly, tears always rimming her eyes. Together they told me the story of the frustrating impasse they had reached with Jody.

"Our understanding with Jody about the finances of his college couldn't have been more clearly spelled out," his father said. "We would pay his tuition and a generous allowance each month that would include money for his room rent, since he wanted to live off campus. But soon he began to say the amount wasn't enough and asked for more. I asked him to tell me where the money was going, and he resisted itemizing it. He would accuse me of not trusting him."

"At first I told Bill to send him the money," Jody's mother said, "but I didn't like it. I knew he was always too free with money. We probably spoiled him a lot."

"And I knew that he was probably spending it on grass and alcohol and who knows what else. So, after sending him some extra money the first couple of times, I put my foot down and said no, he had to live within our agreement. He called in a rage, accusing us of not caring about him or understanding him. A few weeks later he called again, saying he would be thrown out on the street because he hadn't paid his rent. He put his landlord on the phone to confirm it. I still wanted to stand firm, but she said she wouldn't be able to sleep nights."

"It was embarrassing, besides making us worry," Jody's mother recalled. "So I insisted we send him the additional money, telling him it's not to happen again. But of course it did. So the next time we paid the rent directly to the landlord and deducted it from his allowance. He blew his top, calling us collect to scream about how he didn't have enough money and how it proved that we don't care about him. He said we don't love him and never did. He threatened that he wouldn't come home for Easter vacation, and we didn't hear from him for weeks. I couldn't take that. Then he did come home for vacation as if nothing had happened. He brought two friends with him and took it for granted I would feed them. And that was fine with me, in a way, just to have him home."

Jody's father interrupted. "I wouldn't have minded if he acted respectfully toward us and accepted the ground rules of the house, but he didn't, and every time I tried to set him straight, he would get furious and practically insult us in front of his friends. . . . He took my car without permission, smashed it up, and was angry that I was upset about it. He seems to feel that any time we don't let him have his way, it means we don't love him, that we're wanting to hurt him—particularly his mother. It would be hard to find a better mother anywhere, but that always got to her."

"It makes me feel guilty," his mother said, "even though I'm sure I do love him. And I worry about what he's doing to himself and whether I'll make him worse, so I back down and give in."

Better Now Than Never

A woman sat at the wheel of her unmoving car, waiting for a chance to enter the flow of the fast-moving highway traffic. Several minutes went by, and she could not find the right moment to move. Then an exasperated driver in the car behind her stuck his head out of the window and yelled, "Look lady, you'll have to cut the cord sometime."

Whether your child's dependency takes the form of passive clinging, persistent requests or aggressive demands, as long as you give in to it, you are not cutting the cord, you are continuing the old Song and Dance. And continuing it can be devastating for both you and your child. The fact is, *ending a dependent Song and Dance is good parenting. But ending it can be difficult for you because it can feel like bad parenting.*

I saw this conflict clearly with Jody's parents. I encouraged them to take a strong stand with him, to hold firm about the money no matter what the coercion, and to urge Jody to get counseling at college. They agreed it would be best but said it would be hard for them to do this, and they canceled further sessions with me. Months later they came to see me again, this time with Jody. He had flunked out of college, come home, and was now a sullen, hostile presence in the house, not working, not making plans, coming and going at odd hours. All three sat in my office looking bitter, angry and trapped. Clearly, going along with Jody's demands had accomplished nothing good.

Most parents agree that giving in to inappropriate dependency is a bad idea. They can see how destructive the Song and Dance is. Why, then, is it often so difficult to end it? Usually, there is a combination of reasons. For one thing, many parents define their parenting job as "one of nurturing and giving, a continuation of the early years," and they have either never grasped or have lost sight of the fact that nurturing is just one aspect of their essential task, which is to launch their child into independent orbit. A crucial part of this launching is to be able to say, This you may not do, this I will not do. Erma Bombeck, fantasizing about what she would like to tell her children at some time in the future about their accusations that she doesn't love them, ends with, "But most of all, I loved you enough to say no when you hated me for it. That was the hardest part of all."*

Another factor that makes it hard for parents to say no to dependency is their guilt. Very often, they are aware that they contributed to the problem and feel they now have no right to withdraw. One mother said, "I made my daughter lean on me, so how can I pull back now, knowing that she'll probably fall on her face and it would be all my fault?" This is a persistent worry. And indeed your grown-up child may fall on his face, but this is often not as bad as the alternative. Your awareness that you have something to do with your child's failure to be more independent can be helpful in making you deal with the issue more sensitively, more compassionately. *But sensitivity and compassion do not require you to surrender to the emotional blackmail coming from the child.* ("It's your fault so you owe me") or to the guilt coming from inside yourself ("I failed so I owe him"). I have seen par-

* Erma Bombeck, *If Life Is a Bowl of Cherries, What Am I Doing in the Pits?* (New York: McGraw-Hill, 1978), p. 196.

ents who twist their own lives out of shape under the pounding of this combination of blackmail and guilt. I recall a widowed mother who delayed remarriage to a man she cared about because her twenty-five-year-old dependent son didn't like the man and threatened to "run away and never come back" if she did marry. She jeopardized and almost destroyed her relationship with this man before she was able to assert her own needs.

And Jody's parents each had a taut string of guilt that Jody plucked with great skill. His mother had always desperately wanted to be a perfect mother, and to her this had meant centering her life totally around his needs. But she was aware that while she was involved with striving to be her image of the perfect mother, she was not naturally and sensitively attuned to this particular child. She often felt she didn't understand him and his feelings, and she responded by trying even harder to meet his every expressed whim. This combination of pampering and emotional deprivation spurred Jody angrily to demand more and more and led to his mother's feeling helpless to meet his needs. They entered a repetitive and exhausting interaction on this anger-guilt theme. And what about Jody's father? One thing Jody's father knew about himself was that he could be harsh and authoritarian (like his own father, whom he despised), and he often would back down from taking a strong position with Jody for fear of being despotic. Jody, sensing this, would often accuse his father of being unfair and dictatorial, even at times responding to his father's edicts by shouting, "Heil Hitler." Jody thus had learned to manipulate the areas of guilty vulnerability of both his parents in the service of his dependency.

Such guilty soft spots, as well as misunderstandings of the parental role, play their part in undermining the parents' ability to say no to their dependent children. But the primary reason parents have trouble standing firm is because their own inner child is hooked into some kind of Song and Dance with their son or daughter. Parents whose adult offspring are leaning on them, making demands for excessive emotional or financial support, insisting that they be taken care of, and trying to have special exceptions made for them as if they were still little kids are usually afraid that if they stop giving in to those needs, their children will turn against them and turn away from them. In other words, the inner child of the parents is terrified that he or she will be abandoned if they stop meeting their offspring's needs and, as we have seen, no prospect is more terrifying. Conversely, for that inner child no prospect is more enticing and desirable than to hold tightly to their offspring (as if their offspring were the parent).

Thus, the little girl in the mother or the little boy in the father may enter into collusion with their son or daughter to keep the dependent tie intact even while complaining bitterly about it. A parent in such a Song and Dance is at war with himself, his mature parental judgment telling him he must stand firm and risk his offspring's hatred, anger, and possible desertion for the sake of his own and his offspring's independence and growth, while the child within him screams out with terror over these risks.

The parental inner child enters the picture in still another way. Since standing firm with a dependent adult child can often mean taking drastic measures, such as removing support, parents can become very concerned about what others will think if they take such a seemingly harsh stand. Jody's mother explained their yielding to Jody by saying, "I was afraid that if we didn't send him the money, he'd be out on the street, and then what would my parents think?" The little girl in Jody's mother, who had long been determined to try to win her own parents' approval by being a perfect mother, could not bear hearing them say, "How could you let him get thrown out like that?" The needs of this little girl would often win out over her adult maternal judgment. And the need of the little boy in Jody's father to avoid his wife's anger at him was one of the factors that made him unable to sustain a strong stand.

Cord Cutting

If you have a grown-up son or daughter who's still leaning on you as a big source of his emotional and financial supplies, before you can do anything else, you must recognize that this is truly a problem, and a very serious one. It can be so easy to delude yourself about its being a matter of "close family ties," and after all, what's wrong with that?

Certainly, nothing is wrong with close family ties. They are an incomparable source of pleasure and rootedness and sustenance. That is not what we are talking about here. Adult sons and daughters can be independent, effective people, busily engaged in the business of creating lives for themselves and still maintain close family ties. What we are talking about here is the type of dependent closeness that is preventing your adult child from being independent, effective and self-creative. What we are talking about is when the little child in your offspring is hooked almost umbilically to you in a way that proclaims, like Peter Pan, "I don't want to grow up." What we are talking about is the little child *inside yourself* who likes that cozy arrangement and not only motivates you to continue it, but to blind yourself from seeing its destructive nature.

To determine if your child does have a problem of dependency and whether you are both caught up in a Song and Dance, you will have to ask yourself many questions.

Is the amount of contact my child has with me appropriate to his age and status in the world? Does he seem to need to phone me a lot, to see me a lot? And does this seem to be the result of his enjoyment of the contact or out of his feeling lost and abandoned or guilty and anxious if he does not? Can I easily tolerate less contact if he seems to need more space for his own independent development, or do I get anxious or depressed and try to make him feel he is hurting me and letting me down?

Is it really appropriate for someone my child's age to be living with me? How come he is still living with me? Does it really make sense, or is he afraid of going out into the world? And do I really like his living with me so much that I discourage his going out into the world?

Do I honestly believe it is appropriate for someone my child's age to be as financially dependent as he is? Does it fit in with my concept and timetable for financial independence?

Is my adult child able to work effectively, to make independent decisions, to assert himself appropriately, to advance his career, to establish a life that is full and viable?

Is my child able to establish close friendships and to make and sustain love relationships? Do I really want him to, or am I threatened by it?

If my child is married, is he able to stand in the marriage fully, with both feet, committed lovingly to the other person? That commitment must come before his commitment to me if the marriage is to be a good one. Does it? Do I really want it to?

An honest self-survey of these kinds of questions may help you deal with whatever blind spots have kept you from recognizing un unhealthy dependency. But I assume that somewhere inside you, you know that such a problem exists, or you wouldn't be reading this chapter. In fact, your most likely concern would be, If my child is too dependent on me, what can I do about it?

Essentially, you must now do the task that was not successfully completed in the past: Encourage and bring about your child's separation and independence. But as in many developmental tasks whose completion was not accomplished at the optimum time, it will now present many new and upsetting difficulties. There are the years of prolonged expectations on your child's part that you will take care of things. There are the years of your habitually doing so. A pattern has been formed that tends to have a life of its own. To move to change it now is a move toward disruption, and it is often more tempting to choose the familiar but stifling harmony than chance the unknown emotional earthquake that could emanate from such a disruption. Yet I must urge you to end the dependent Song and Dance because it is crippling for both you and your child. Ending the old arrangement often involves proclaiming a new contract and then taking a firm stand on it.

It can be awfully hard to tell a grown-up child who is living with you to move out. But if it is beyond that point where it is good for either of you, beyond that point where he or she could be financially self-sufficient, beyond the point where most people his age are living on their own, or with others, or are married, then you must encourage him to make this move. Sensitivity to his dependence on you and his fear of being out there on his own may lead you to give him emotional support, to set up a reasonable timetable, to assure him of your caring. And if he still has that much resistance to it, that much fear of it, it is important to suggest that he alone or all of you as a family get professional counseling because the problem is obviously a very difficult one. Sooner or later you will have to say, "Sorry, this cannot go on.

You must move out. Neither you nor we can grow in this arrangement." Then you must firmly and strongly *insist* on it and take whatever steps are necessary to bring it about.

It is not only on issues of living with you that such a stand must be taken, for many of you have children who are dependent though no longer sharing the house. The issue can be, "Sorry, we will be giving you no more money. You will have to manage on you own." Or, "Sorry, as much as I love my grandchild, you cannot count on us for regular baby-sitting. You will have to make other arrangements." No matter what the issue, the principle is always the same: Whenever your best judgment tells you that the present pattern is stunting the growth of your child's capacity to manage alone in the world without you, you will have to get him out of the actual or symbolic nest one way or the other.

Taking this kind of stand will often put you in conflict not only with your offspring but with yourself. The child within you may be crying out, "Don't do it. You'll lose him. He'll be angry. He'll be hurt. He won't be able to manage. He'll hate you. He'll have nothing to do with you." And that can be a compelling voice, difficult to override. Besides, you will be up against all your feelings that a good parent doesn't say no to his child's demands to be taken care of. And there may be voices of your own parents saying you are bad for saying no.

It will therefore take considerable courage for you to withstand the promptings of your offspring, your inner child fears and needs, and the possible criticism you may receive when you take a stand against your child's dependency demands. Your inner conflict may often cause you to give double messages:

> "You will have to move out, but you can have all the time you need."
>
> "I refuse to give you one more cent unless you absolutely need it."
>
> "I won't be baby-sitting for you anymore, but if you're stuck, call me."
>
> "You will have to start contributing to the household, but first save some money for a rainy day."

The first part of the statement comes from your parental judgment and reflects your attempts to put realistic limits on the dependence, while the second part most probably comes from your inner child, frightened that you have gone too far. The double message is, "I want you to stand on your own two feet, but lean on me."

In taking a courageous stand, it is nice to have an ally, so it is enormously helpful if your spouse agrees with the need for such a stand, and you can offer each other support in sustaining it. Often, this is not the case, and you will have to present as clearly as possible your reasons for taking your position, to find that part in your spouse that agrees with you, and to support that part of your spouse against the pull of his own inner child. (If it is your spouse who is in favor of taking a stronger stand, listen to him very carefully, trying to respond with your most mature parental judgment and not your needy inner child. If you agree with him, try to gain from his determination and support him with your strength.) For example, Jody's father was able to say to his wife, "Let's give Jody two weeks to move out. I know it's hard for you and it's hard for me, too. But we both know it's for the best, and we can help each other with it." And they did stand together, and Jody did take a makeshift job to support his moving into an apartment with a friend, a job that led to a better job and the beginnings of a calmer and more relaxed relationship with his parents than ever before.

It is not always obvious when it is appropriate to take a stand and when it is not. A husband and wife, each in their mid-sixties, were eager and prepared to retire to a home they had bought in a warm climate when their son announced that his marriage was breaking up, there might be a long and nasty conflict around his children, he was very shattered and shaky, and he'd like them to delay going away for at least several months. They decided to do so. The father said, "Stan has always been a very independent boy. If he's asking for help, then I know he really needs it, and I'm glad to be there for him. If he were one of those kids I know who are always leaning on their parents, I might feel, Here we go again, and not do it."

I might add that if his son were one of those kids who was always leaning on his parents, it might be better for him that his parents not give in to this request, as cruel as that may seem. (In general, genuine life crises are not good times to withdraw support. But some adult children can create one crisis after another so that you will never find a good time if you keep delaying.) Whenever you stand up to a child's inappropriate dependency demand, you will be helping him assume his birthright as an independently functioning, growing and strong adult. You will be helping him discover capacities in himself that he never exercised. There is the joke about the teen-age boy who had always been mute. His doting parents had taken him to every kind of specialist and clinic, but nothing wrong could be found with his speech organs or hearing. Then one day, while at dinner, he spoke up clearly and loudly saying, "Please pass the salt." His joyful parents screamed, "You can talk! How come you never spoke before?" The boy looked at them and said, "'Til now, everything was fine."

Not only is there a lot in it for your child if you insist on greater separation and independence, but for yourself. As long as your inner child has you focused primarily around maintaining a tight, constricting bond with your offspring, you cannot grow to your full stature. You are entitled to put down the caretaking aspects of parenting and to stretch yourself and experience the freedom of being first a person and second a parent. And you are entitled to be alone with your spouse and to rediscover the relationship between the two people who came together before there ever was anyone you called your son or your daughter.

It is scary, but you are entitled to it.

CHAPTER 6

If You Go Away

We live in Connecticut in the same house we've been in for over thirty years. My son lives in California, much farther away than my fantasy of what a family would be like. My daughter-in-law is from the West Coast—they lived here for a year and she couldn't take it. Then he got a good job out there. They try to come East once a year and we go out there once. But it's difficult when you see how fast time is running, and we were such a close family. The separation would be okay if it wasn't that far. I saw my grandson only once—it's not satisfying for a grandmother, and it bothers my husband even more.

Parents who themselves may never have lived more than an hour from their own parents, often just down the block, are frequently confronted with their children's moving a continent or an ocean away. As a woman in a discussion group I participated in said, "Don't you think that distance has to be an important difference between our generation and our children and whatever went before? Of the people sitting in this room who each have two or three children old enough to be independent, very few live near enough to come home. So in actual fact, what we're talking about is a closeness or lack of closeness through telephone calls and occasional visits."

This type of geographical distance isn't all that new. Many of today's parents or grandparents left families in other countries, emigrating to find new opportunities. Many left rural areas for the city. Others followed chosen careers or mates to distant points. But the easy transportation of today, the tendency of corporations to transfer their employees to far-flung offices or plants, and the emphasis on finding one's own directions and place make it a common occurrence for children to move out of easy visiting distance of their parents. I read an article by a mother whose daughter Amy and Amy's intended husband announced that after their marriage they planned to emigrate to Israel. She wrote of her reactions and those of her own husband. "Marty and I were growing heartsick at the prospect that our beautiful and wonderful Amy would eventually leave us. One day, while discussing our feelings about Amy's leaving, Marty said, 'I feel gypped from beginning to end. Not to be together for holidays, not to be allowed the pleasure of fondling my grandchild or watching him grow up is more than I can bear.' Then the wedding was over, and we were compelled to face the fact that our children's departure was imminent. I found myself unable to sleep at night and would awaken in the morning with tears in my eyes. At work, I would think about the children's departure and find myself crying. Marty was silent, too pent up with his own emotional dilemma to accept the inevitable."* (We'll get back to Amy's mother later.)

So Near but So Far

Not all parental complaints about distance involve mileage. In fact, I know of instances where much sharing and closeness is retained despite hours or days of travel time between the parent and offspring, while light years of cold space can exist between parents and a child in the same home or living close by. And this kind of distance can be even more painful for the parents.

* Gert Landis, "When a Child Makes Aliyah," *Reform Judaism*, May 1978, p. 5.

> Penny used to talk to me about everything, and now she calls every few months. She makes it clear that my calls are unwelcome. And she lives just downtown. I can't take it.
>
> Philip said that for now he can't handle being in touch with me. Those were his words, "I can't handle it." He said that maybe later, when he gets things together in his own head he'll be able to. It's been over two years, and I've gotten two birthday cards and a phone call when he heard I was laid up with phlebitis.

Why does a child set a course that intentionally takes him far out of hailing distance from the people with whom he once was so intensely intertwined?

Somewhere in that journey from symbiotic attachment to independence, something went awry and prevented him from attaining that desirable state of being separate from them, yet remaining in caring touch with them. Sometimes parents can feel this distance growing when the children are still quite young. One mother of four spoke of her oldest and youngest children, both sons: "They're two absolutely opposite personalities. The younger one keeps everything to himself—whether he lets it out somewhere else, I don't know. He's very much a closed-mouth type of person, while the older one is very sensitive, very emotional. You know right away what he's feeling. . . . One day I realized there was hardly any physical contact between us anymore—when they're grown-up you don't touch them. So I said, 'Every night before you go to sleep, I want a hug and a kiss.' The older one always does; the younger one never remembers. He'll say goodnight and I'll have to call him back and say, 'You forgot something,' and he'll walk back and he'll give it to me, but it's Okay, yeah, gotta do this again, with a little bit of annoyance. . . . The older one, whomever he marries, if he lives in any close vicinity to where we are living, will be close. The younger one may pick himself up and go to the other end of the country, and we'll see him once a year. And even if he doesn't go far, if he lives two towns away, it'll be very much of, I have to visit my parents on Sunday afternoon type of thing. I feel hurt, hurt."

If your child is distancing you, you may wonder, as did this mother, why one child will be open and another so guarded. There are several factors that go into the development of an emotionally distant child, some of them going back to the first months of his life. In some instances, there are innate or very early differences in how much emotional excitation a particular infant can take, because infants differ widely in their ability to cope with stimuli. The young child's brand new neurogical and physiological apparatus must cope with the innumerable happenings that William James called "that buzzing, blooming confusion." If he were to respond to each with equal intensity, he would become too disorganized to function. To help in this he has a "stimulus barrier," a way of blocking out or muting sensory input to make the world handleable. When a child has a "thin" stimulus barrier, he may experience a loud noise, a delayed meal, a scolding, a wet diaper, mother's bad mood or mother's hugging much more painfully or intensely than another child, and he may develop ways to keep other people at an actual or emotional distance in order to protect himself from disturbing or overwhelming feelings. He may begin to keep to himself or keep his feelings and thoughts to himself.

In addition to these biological factors, there is the child's early world which, to a great extent, is his parents. And just as Heraclitus said that no man can step into the same river twice because the second time it is not the same river or the same man, no two children can be born into the same family, whether they arrive five years or five minutes apart. The way he is received, his parents' feelings about him, the family constellation at the time (and I have seen twins where the one born five minutes sooner is ever after treated as the "older one"), the family finances, the age of his parents, what's happening in the marriage, the feelings and expectations his parents have of him, etc., present a novel environment for each offspring. The way particular parents interact with a particular and uniquely put together child will have a lot to do with whether he will be open to them or will shut himself off from them.

For example, if a child does have that thin stimulus barrier we spoke of, when stimuli impinge on him with great force, a parent who is tuned in to this in his child will sense the importance of functioning as a "supplementary stimulus barrier," as someone who eases the impact of the world's sights and sounds and emotions, thus enabling him to deal with the world effectively rather than to feel overwhelmed by it. Parents who are not empathetically tuned in, who buffet such a child with stimuli rather than buffer him from them, may find that their children retreat from other people, bury their emotions and are unable to be close or intimate—it's been too painful. Even with children whose stimulus barrier is effective, the parents who are tuned in and responsive to the unique psychological and physiological make-up of the particular child are more likely to find that their child is open with them than those who are not.

If you have children who are adults, all this is ancient history, and these early events that made your child distant cannot be undone. But this perspective can help you to look back and determine whether his withdrawal from you was a very early one or if it came about later, perhaps in his adolescence or young adulthood. If his withdrawal was very early and you fail to recognize the profound self-protective needs it has served, you are more likely to be propelled by angry and hurt feelings to get into a destructive Song and Dance with him, trying, with great frustration to each of you, to get him to end a very deeply entrenched pattern.

Often, the origins of this distancing are not so early but come out of later developments in the relationship. For example, Philip, the young man whose mother quoted him as saying about contact with her, "I just can't handle it," later told me, "I used to be the typical good boy, you might even say a mama's boy. As I began to gain more self-confidence and wanted to be more independent, it would lead to terrible fights. Both my parents would accuse me of not loving them. They would try to order me to be there when they wanted me, and I would get furious and say some pretty nasty things. I would try to explain that I was not against them but had my own life to lead, but they'd still try to control when and how often I'd see them. I couldn't stand the anger and guilty feelings. So I told them I had to keep away from them. I got an unlisted phone and refused to receive their calls at work. It's unfortunate, but I sure couldn't go on the other way."

What Philip is describing is an attempt to end an old Song and Dance. This Song and Dance was originally between dependent little Philip (who wanted his parents' loving approval and had learned that by always doing what they wanted, he could get it) and the controlling child in each parent (who was afraid that Philip would abandon him if he had his own separate pursuits). Then, when Philip asserted his wish for more independence, a new Song and Dance developed between the autonomy-seeking, rebellious Philip and the enraged, bossy little child in each parent. Philip found it just as disturbing to live with the upsetting and destructive emotions of the defiant Song and Dance as with the suffocating feelings of the compliant one. So his distancing was an attempt to end the old Songs and Dances by withdrawing from most interaction with his parents. *Often a child's distancing is just that, an attempt to end a way of relating that he can no longer tolerate.*

In other instances, the distancing may not be an attempt to end a Song and Dance but may be in itself a *new* Song and Dance. Beneath a seeming withdrawal from the old gavotte, his cutting you off can be an expression of enormous anger, the child within your child saying, All right for you. Distancing can be one of the most powerful punishments a child can give to his parents. It can be an extension of some of the earliest war maneuvers children use with their parents such as the silent treatment, sulking, and running away from home. Penny, the young woman whose mother spoke of not being able to take it that Penny, who once was close but now rarely made contact with them, said, "Let them stew in their own juices. Maybe if they come crawling I'll speak to them."

If your child is distancing you, it can be difficult to differentiate if he is a somewhat withdrawn person who finds most relationships difficult and distasteful, or if he is trying to end a Song and Dance, thus inviting you to a new, more mature and peerlike interaction, or if he is doing a new variation on an old Song and Dance theme. And you also have to consider the possibility that unfortunately, he may be a shallow, self-involved, even selfish individual who wants little in the way of obligations, responsibilities or inconveniences. One man of twenty-five who cut off most contact with his parents explained, "I just don't want the hassle."

Why Did He Go Away?

It will be helpful to understand as well as you can why your son or daughter decided to cut himself off from you. There are many questions to ask yourself, questions about him and questions about yourself. First, let's look at your son or daughter:

—Is he basically a "loner" who dislikes the demands and impingements of other people?

—Does he need to keep close relationships with others minimal in order to maintain a shaky equilibrium and to keep from feeling disorganized by the demands of life?

—Is he too narcissistic and self-centered to sustain relationships and to maintain commitments when they are no longer necessary to gratify his own needs?

—Is he still so much a child that he must "pick up his marbles and go home" when he doesn't get everything his own way?

—Is he so selfish that he will not inconvenience himself or put himself out to meet your needs and would rather cut you off than do so?

Now, let's look at you. It's important that you confront yourself with these questions:

—Do you have something to do with his decision to be distant? What? What Songs and Dances may you have engaged in with him?

—Have you made yourself unwelcome by trying to control him too much? By trying to set the terms of the relationship? By intruding into his life?

—Or have you disappointed him too often by not being there for him when he wanted you to be? By not being sensitive to his need for your support so that he is now determined not to leave himself open to that disappointment again?

—Has there been so much arguing and conflict that it has become just too aggravating for him to be with you?

—Have you complained so much about your pains, suffering and unhappiness that you have made yourself too unpleasant to be around?

—Have you provoked guilt by making him feel that he is a big cause of your suffering?

—Have you criticized him so much that he has come to feel, Who needs this?

There may not be much you can do about those motivations in your son or daughter that arise out of his own internal conflicts and his own personality. But understanding the inner roots of his distancing will make a difference in how you will respond. If you see him as protecting the functioning of a self so fragile that it can easily be disrupted by the emotional requirements of a relationship, your feelings are likely to be more compassionate and even supportive of his need for distance than if you see him as selfishly or hostilely disregarding you and your feelings. And the stance you take with him will then inevitably be different.

If you see that there are aspects of you and of your actions that have made it hard for him to maintain a relationship with you and try to understand why you have acted that way and begin to change it, then your child's responses may shift. It is certainly difficult to communicate that you have changed when your offspring is hardly talking to you, but there will probably be instances, even in brief and sporadic contacts, in which that change will be apparent to him. The very vibrations you emit and the atmosphere you create may signal your child that something new has happened, that you are no longer relating in the way he found intolerable. Of course, if your child has ended *all* contact with you, it will be nearly impossible to get that message across. But even then, sending a letter that openly conveys "I can see what I was doing that made you cut yourself off from me, and I'd like to show you that things can be different" is more likely to get a positive reception than a letter that criticizes, blames or provokes guilt.

Your Abandoned Inner Child

If your child has drastically reduced the amount and quality of his contact with you, it is deeply frustrating if you have expected, as most parents do, that your offspring would be a source of mutual caring and involvement for the rest of your days. It is an understandable wish, and its thwarting is disappointing even to the mature parenting part of you that has fostered your child's separateness. When Mel Brooks in his record "The 2,000 Year Old Man" complains to Carl Reiner, "I have 42,000 children and none of them comes to visit me," it is funny, but when we're talking of your son or daughter, it can be a heartache. And what makes your distress particularly upsetting is that he or she had made a reality of the greatest fear of your inner child, the fear of abandonment. If your offspring is in a state of active, angry conflict with you, the *threat* of abandonment is always hovering, but he has not abandoned you. In fact the anger itself binds you together. But when you repeatedly ask your son or daughter to visit and get a cool refusal, when you pick up the ringing phone hopefully but never hear his voice, when you call him and as you try to engage him are left holding a dead line, then the child who lives within you will scream out like a child just orphaned by war, sitting alone in the road.

It's going to be hard coming to terms with your cut-off son or daughter while you are so upset. So the first priority must go to recognizing your own abandoned inner child. That child is there —just let your feelings of pain and anger about your cut-off son or daughter well up in you, and you will find that child. Then let yourself have an image of that howling child inside you. Picture picking up and comforting him. What would you say? I once treated a forty-four-year-old woman named Margaret. She had a daughter, Cindy, who had recently been married. The marriage had aroused a lot of conflict between this mother and her daughter which got worse when Cindy and her new husband decided to move 1,800 miles away. Shortly after the move and after a few stressful arguments on the phone, Cindy sent a letter to her mother saying that she wished to have very little to do with her for now and asking her not to write or call. Margaret went into a panic. Her feelings would go from fury to bottomless depression and back to fury. I asked her to picture the abandoned child within herself. She saw herself as about three years old, crying hysterically in her crib with nobody coming to comfort her. I asked her to imagine that she would pick baby Margaret up and tell her what she needed to hear. Margaret felt too self-conscious to do it in my office, so she said she would write a letter to her inner child at home. She wrote:

> Dear little Margaret,
>
> I know how dreadful you feel, like it's the end of the world. But it isn't you know because you still have me, and I love you. Cindy has left us, maybe for a little while, maybe for always. I know to you it seems like for always and you won't be able to stand it. But the pain will get much less. I know because I've lived a long time and know about such things, and you're just a scared little girl. . . . Anyhow, we both have a big life. There's Jack and he's really a good man. And there are all our friends, and our work, and so much to see and do.
>
> It's sad about Cindy, and I hope it won't always be that way, but we didn't always have Cindy, remember? We went twenty-one years without her, and we did just fine. So believe me, you'll be all right. I promise I'll take good care of you. I promise.

As Margaret got stronger and less frantic about Cindy's cutting off contact, she approached her again in an open and reasonable way, which brought a cautious but positive response.

So before you can take more constructive steps, you must comfort that sad and angry child inside you. The mature you must let your inner child know what it does not know—that it's not the end of the world, that life can go on and be filled with much richness, excitement and fulfillment even if your grown-up son or daughter has largely cut himself off from you.

Dealing with the Distance

If you don't come to terms with your own inner child, if you don't come to see your own contribution to your son's or daughter's withdrawal from you, then you run the danger of beginning a new Song and Dance that will only make the situation worse. If you react to your child's withdrawal through martyrdom (Look how you're hurting me, see how you're hurting your father/mother, how can you do this to us), you will probably push your child further away. Who likes to be made to feel bad? If you react to your child's withdrawal with rage (How dare you, you'll be sorry, go to hell) or by being judgmental (You're bad, you're an unnatural child, you're selfish), you will probably push him further away. Who needs that flak? Or if you start a retaliatory Song and Dance (your version of All right for you, which may mean cutting him out of your will or some other reprisal) you may be foreclosing on the possibility of ever narrowing the gap. Besides the fact that such new Songs and Dances will cause more bad feelings in everybody, when a young man or woman cuts himself off from his parents, it is frequently a transient phase in his development, a moratorium in his having been overly involved with them, a time of consolidation of a new sense of self and of choosing a new direction for his life. Frequently, once he has attained this fresh feeling of who he is and feels secure in maintaining his redefined boundaries, he may poke out of his self-imposed retreat, and he may wish to re-establish his link to his parents. If you have reacted to his withdrawal with new and destructive Songs and Dances, you may have made it difficult, if not impossible, for a rebirth of his relationship with you.

I wish I could tell you that if you avoid starting new Songs and Dances by keeping your needy inner child out of the interaction and responding from the mature parent part of yourself, your offspring will definitely accept your invitation to a revitalized relationship. He probably will, but he may not. His contribution to the problem may have always been and may continue to be a self-centeredness or a need to avoid the upsetting impingements, infringements and inconveniences of an active relationship. So one of your goals in coming to terms with your cut-off offspring will have to be the *acceptance of his need for the distance he is putting there and of his right to put it there*.

Acceptance does not mean liking it. It does not mean that you must stop trying to reach out and to communicate directly and clearly your wish for more contact and the *mature* needs it comes out of—caring and a wish for continuity. But it does mean accepting that beyond that, there is nothing more you can do. Your child, for whatever reason, chooses to keep away from you. He is old enough to make that choice and self-maintaining enough to enforce his wishes. There may be selfishness in it. There may be meanness in it. But he *can* do it. And if you feel that his distancing is directed *against* you, or that it is too painful and frustrating to go on as it is, you may wish to end any further attempts of your own to reach out. You may have come to a saturation point where you don't want such a one-sided relationship. That is *your* right, and it can be a very appropriate though sad position to take.

There are two things to keep in mind that can lift your morale enormously even though the distance may continue. First, your life goes on, and its fulfillment does not depend on how close or how unavailable your son or daughter is.

Second, no matter what other motives have gone into your child's decision to withdraw and whether the distancing is geographical, emotional or both, you can be sure that at least part of his motivation derives from a healthy wish to be a freestanding adult, and that can make you respect him and feel pride in yourself for having been successful at that essential parenting task of launching him on his own trajectory through life. Remember the mother who was upset about her daughter, Amy, emigrating to Israel? She went on to write, "One day I came to the conclusion that I was allowing myself to wallow in self-pity. I was playing the part of the resentful and angry parent. All the while I was thinking, How could they do this to us? How could they leave us? Surely they don't love us. Suddenly I awakened with a realization. Indeed they could do this to us and, indeed, they must. I realized that if they stayed near us, they would be fulfilling *our* desires and not their own destiny. Individuals must live their lives according to what they feel is right. Children must ultimately make their own way and be independent people, free and separate from the nurturing parental influence. I then realized how difficult the departure must be for them. It's much easier to be the protected child rather than the independent adult."*

* Gert Landis, "When A Child Makes Aliyah."

This recognition of the positive aspect of the distancing was also reflected in the words of a mother who rarely had contact with her daughter but knew she was happily married and was advancing successfully in her career as a TV writer. She said with a sigh, "I must have done something right."

CHAPTER 7

Strange Music in My Ears

Not too long ago, when children came of age, they chose one of a small number of roads that forked off and usually paralleled the main parental turnpike. It was even easier then for parents to let go because they could feel assured that their children would take paths that were familiar, that ran nearby, and that probably led to places that they, the parents, had mapped long ago. But now, the alternative roads are countless, and the offspring veer off their parents' well-marked routes precipitously, heading into territory as strange and exotic as Xanadu, as cold and lunar as Patagonia, as wrong and sinful as Sodom. Even for parents who understand that their children must go their own ways, it is hard to let go if it means losing them in the void.

Disappointed Expectations

What is this void? It is a new and in many ways unrecognizable world, a world that has known metamorphosing earthquakes since you, the parents, were the same age your children are now. These changes in the social landscape, which probably make your view of what is appropriate behavior different from your child's view, can be placed into three categories:

1. Sex
2. Marriage and Family
3. Unconventional Life-styles

All of these areas of social change are potential areas for intergenerational conflict and disappointed parental expectations. We will approach each through the words, almost the lamentations, of some distressed parents.

SEX

My daughter is living with her boyfriend. I can't get used to it. The idea of her sleeping with someone she's not married to, day in and day out, so rubs me the wrong way that I can't really deal with it. At first I argued with her and I was furious. Now I try to ignore it. I think if I had ever done that, my parents would have killed me or disowned me.

There are few areas in which the changes have been greater in so short a period of time than in sexual attitudes and behavior. You grew up in a world where the accepted ground rules and experiences of your family and friends now contrast sharply with the accepted standards and experiences of your children.

I remember we had to get girls back to their dormitories at 10 P.M., *1* A.M. *on weekends. And no boys were permitted above the first-floor lounge. The lounge would be filled with couples kissing goodnight. Now my daughter is at the same college, sharing the same dormitory with boys, even using the same bathrooms!*

That was the reminiscence of a father who had just returned from visiting his daughter at his old alma mater.

A mother of four children, ranging in age from seventeen to twenty-five, said:

How terrified we all were of pregnancy. I recall that at times my period was late out of anxiety about being pregnant when the most we ever did was pet! My kids don't think twice about getting pregnant, although I'm sure they have active sex lives. They don't have to worry about it.

What caused such momentous changes in so short a time? A combination of factors: Some are technological, like the development of the contraceptive pill and other forms of pregnancy control. Others are legal, such as the increased availability of abortion. Many are sociological, such as the increased acceptance of unmarried couples and the growing demand of women for equality in every sphere, including the right to seek equal sexual fulfillment. And there are educational factors, such as the dissemination of sexual knowledge to help people find joy and more joy in lovemaking.

All these trends have set the stage for potential conflict between you and your child. Whereas you may have grown up believing that men wouldn't respect women who are "easy," your children have grown up believing that men may question what kind of neurotic sexual hang-up a woman has if she's too "difficult." Whereas you grew up believing that for a woman to live with a man she was not married to was immoral and imprudent, your children have grown up feeling that it is both pleasurable and practical for couples to live with each other either before getting married or with no intention of getting married.

These differences are so great, and so pervasive, that parents who have no flexibility in this area run the risk of a serious rift with their children. The rift can take the form of continuous, angry disputes or a rupture of contact. Often it leads the children to live a hidden life, lying and covering up so that this important area of life is in no way shared with their parents. Most parents accommodate to these changes in sexual mores. In fact, some parents, particularly if they feel that their child is too young to settle down or don't like his choice, will now say, "You don't have to get married right away. Why don't you live with each other and see how it goes?" Increasing numbers of parents are saying this to their children, while they can't possibly picture their own parents as saying anything like it to them when they were younger.

In the novel *Evergreen,* Anna has joined her granddaughter Laura in France where Laura was on a hosteling trip. They are to do some traveling together. At the hotel, Laura lets her grandmother know that she has been traveling with a boy all summer. The next morning Anna watches as:

> Laura opens her eyes and blinks into glorious light. Her skin is moist and pink with sleep, like a baby's when he wakes from his nap. And that boy, Anna thinks, that boy sees her like this every morning, takes it as his right, as if he owned her! Anna is outraged at the boldness of him and outraged at Laura.
>
> "Fool! Fool! Wrecking your life when you have everything and are too stupid to know you have it." *

Much later on, after they have had a wonderful trip together, Laura asks her grandmother if she has been angry about it.

> Anna turns to her. "I was. But I'm not anymore."
>
> "Why not?"
>
> "It just went away, the anger, hurt or whatever you want to call it. . . . "
>
> As always, Anna sees both sides of the question. . . . She knows one thing, though, that you can't live by slogans. What's honest for one is a lie to another.
>
> "The main thing is to live. Foster life. Cherish it. Plant flowers and if you can't pull the weeds up, hide them." †

There will be areas of change in sexual practices that some parents will not be able to accommodate. One of the most common questions I hear from parents is something like this: "My daughter is living with a boy at college. They're very close. This summer they'll be spending time with us at our country place, and I know I simply couldn't take their sleeping in the same room in my house. I know it's not logical, it's even hypocritical, and I've tried to adjust to the idea the way I adjusted to her living with him at school, but I can't." There is no reason for parents to put themselves through such discomfort and distress. The dif-

* Belva Plain, *Evergreen* (New York: Delacorte, 1978), p. 569.

† *Ibid.*, p. 572.

ferences in background and codes are very real and emotionally charged, and you have every right to say, "I'm sorry, I can understand that you might feel this makes no sense, but I am too uncomfortable about your sharing a room and a bed together in this house, and I want you to respect my feelings about it."

It is not too much for you to ask. Consideration involves respecting other people's discomforts, and consideration or requesting consideration is never out of place. There will be some discomfort involved for your children in this, but they have choices ranging from abiding by your wishes completely, to getting together discreetly, to going elsewhere. Only you can know when you have reached the point where you have accommodated all that you can without doing violence to some important part of yourself. And where you and your spouse disagree on this issue, when you've discussed it thoroughly and have had ample opportunity to convince each other, if one of you still feels uncomfortable about it, it is considerate for the other to go along. In essence, you would say to your children, "If it were up to me alone, I'd let you share the room, but your father's (mother's) feelings are very important to me, and I would like you, too, to respect them."

Another issue confronting a small but sizable percentage of parents is the discovery that their child is homosexual. This is more of an issue than ever because as part of the sexual revolution and civil liberties struggle, homosexuality is coming out of the closet a bit more frequently. The awareness that their child is gay is often so outside anything in the parents' expectations that the initial reaction is often one of shock, horror, anger and an attempt to talk their child out of it. Many parents feel it to be not only a tragic development for their child, but something weak, shameful, immoral and an abomination. How do they reconcile these feelings with their love for their own child?

I recall watching a program on the Phil Donahue television show where the guests were members of a group called "Parents of Gays," parents who had banded together to help each other come to terms with the problems of having gay children. The studio audience seemed hostile to these parents' acceptance of the homosexuality of their own children. Then a man phoned in and told the story of his awareness as a child that he was gay and his unsuccessful attempts to fight it. He told of a morning when he was a young man, miserable and so desperate to share his secret that he spoke to his mother about it. The same day she phoned his father who went to see his lawyer, and by that night he was legally disowned. The audience gasped, and that gasp was what most impressed me. The audience, who had been so disdainful of homosexuals and their parents, reacted instantly with shock and dismay at hearing this man talk of being disowned by those who brought him into the world, raised him and presumably loved him. Perhaps many in the audience had not realized until that moment the ultimate human consequences of living out that prejudice.

If you have a child who is gay, you too may find it hard to make an accommodation. If so, there are two questions you might ask yourself:

1. Might not my strong feelings of outrage grow out of my inner child, out of old learning placed in my head so long ago that I have never truly questioned them with my now greater knowledge, wisdom and compassion?

2. Are those inner-child demands that my son or daughter live according to my wishes and expectations preventing me from giving him the love and support which he may especially need if he is traveling a hard and lonely road?

MARRIAGE AND FAMILY

My daughter is twenty-nine and she's single. Not that she isn't attractive; she's a lovely girl. But she tells me she has no desire to be married now and maybe never. She says she loves being free and loves her work—she's in advertising —I can't really understand it. It seems like such an empty life, but she avoids marriage like the plague.

While most young people still want to be married, a growing number of men and women are opting to remain single or to remain single longer than in your day. Many things go into it: the increased interest of women in careers and freedom of movement rather than in the obligations and commitments of marriage and homemaking; the lifting of the stigma of spinsterhood or "old maidhood"; the new social structure society has erected for unmarried people, such as singles events, singles bars, singles clubs, singles resorts, singles apartment complexes, etc.; cynicism about marriage based on the high divorce rate and the number of unhappy marriages young people see around them; and the greater acceptance of living together, vacationing together and traveling together by unmarried couples. In your generation, if you did dare to travel with someone you were not married to, you had better sign the hotel register as Mr. and Mrs. Now this is usually unnecessary and unquestioned.

> *My son is married five years and they have no children. Last week I finally asked him if there was something wrong. He said that everything was fine, but they had decided even before marriage that they didn't want children and they still feel the same way. What's marriage without children? Two people are no family.*

Married couples are often waiting longer before having children, are having fewer, and sometimes are choosing to remain childless. Having children usually still goes with being married, but there is a change in attitude so that people can choose to be childless without being universally regarded as strange or selfish. Increasingly, a couple is considered a family with its *raison d'être* in itself and not as a procreational unit. And couples who have one child are not as frequently assailed by others for not giving their child a sibling to play with or to keep him from being spoiled. All the many changes of recent years—women wanting more freedom and careers, men wanting to be less burdened by the role of provider, and contraceptive advances—have contributed to this trend, as well as the economic inflation that makes the decision to have a child a large and mounting financial commitment.

It is understandable that you would want to see your children become parents if you believe it's an important and fulfilling experience for people to have. It is understandable that you would want to be a grandparent, as that is a particular joy you would not want to pass up. And it is understandable that you would want to see the continuity of your family; it is a kind of immortality. But if your children resist having children and have thought it out and have their rationale, even though you may disagree with that rationale, then you have to ask yourself, Do I really want them to have children for them or for me? *There are a few things sadder and more unfair in this world than when a child is brought into it for the wrong reasons, and it would be the wrong reason for your children to bring forth a child in order to please you.* You can let your child know how you feel about it and why you would like it if they had children, but pressing beyond that can either lead to conflict or an unwanted baby or both. If you don't want those unhappy results, you will have to reconcile yourself to not having grandchildren from that child by bringing to bear the mature part of you that knows you can never have all your wishes met. And you can foster your own acceptance of your child's decision if you really respect his judgment and self-knowledge. As one young woman I know said, "What my mother can't understand is that I so despise everything about having a child that I know I'd make a terrible mother. The world doesn't need more children of terrible mothers."

We haven't been deeply religious people. I mean we haven't followed all the traditions and rituals. But still, our children were brought up with it and now, Kenny is marrying someone of a different faith. He has to know how much it is hurting us. It's tearing us both apart. I still haven't told my parents. I think it would kill them. I'm considering not going to the wedding and just letting him go his way. After all, it's his decision, not mine.

Intermarriage—religious, ethnic or racial—has long been a cause of violent and tragic wrenching of the parent-child bond. And with increased mobility and greater emphasis on the pursuit of personal freedom, it is happening more often. The feelings it raises in the parents come in part from the mature part that sees the value in maintaining a heritage and anticipates the potential conflict that may occur for their child with his spouse and with society in general. Marriage is difficult enough, upset parents may feel, why make it harder? But the parent may also have strong reactions stemming from his inner child. The little child in the parent may be afraid he will really lose his son or daughter now that his offspring is entering into a new and foreign alliance. Besides the loss, little children fear whatever is strange, and what they are afraid of they will tend to avoid or attack. And the child within the parent is often very concerned with what his own parent may think and may react more to appease his own parent than to be helpful to his own children.

If your child has married outside your religion or race, and you truly believe that life will be harder for him because of that choice, then wouldn't it be even more important that you, as his parent, help to ease the way? Of course, it depends on the depth of your belief, on the importance of the issue to you. Elsewhere, I have written: *

> How much change a parent can accept in his child is a very individual matter. In the popular musical *Fiddler on the Roof,* Tevye is faced with each of his three daughters choosing paths that differed from his hopes and expectations. First, Tzeitel wants to marry a poor tailor instead of the rich man or scholar he and his wife had wanted for her. Tevye debates with himself, counterbalancing each statement with, "On the other hand . . ." Then Tevye shrugs and says, "Well children, when shall we make the wedding?"
>
> His second daughter, Hodel, wants to marry a radical who is dedicated to the overthrow of the Czar. They don't even ask for his permission, but for his blessing. He is upset, obsessed about "the other hand . . ." and finally concludes, "Very well children, you have my blessing—and my permission."
>
> But when he is told that Chava, his youngest and his favorite, has married a non-Jew it is different. When Chava asks him to accept them he talks to heaven, "Accept them? How can I accept them? Can I deny everything I believe in? On the other hand, can I deny my own child? On the other hand, how can I turn my back on my faith, my people? If I try to bend that far I will break. On the other hand . . . there is no other hand. No, Chava. No—no—no." †

* Howard Halpern, *Cutting Loose,* p. 234.

† Joseph Stein, *Fiddler on the Roof* (New York: Pocket Books, 1966). Based on Sholem Aleichem's stories.

Perhaps you, too, have reached a breaking point where your own core beliefs and values are so challenged that you must make a break of some degree with your child. It is crucial that you make every effort to delineate whether it is really an unacceptable challenge to your belief system or whether the child in you is having a tantrum about not getting his own way, because your decision can have very lasting consequences. In the novel *Evergreen,** when Maury, the golden son of Anna and Joseph Friedman, decides to marry Agatha, a non-Jewish girl, his parents cut off contact with the young couple. And so do Agatha's Wasp parents from Vermont. The young couple find themselves alone, without support or help of any type, just as the Depression of the thirties begins. He is out of work, she becomes pregnant, they are close to starvation, and their life is a nightmare. Maury takes a job running numbers for a racketeer, but by then Agatha, in an attempt to escape her despair, has begun to drink heavily. Maury is brutally beaten by members of an opposing gangster mob, his parents come to the hospital and they reconcile. Life gets better but by now Agatha has become an alcoholic. She and Maury quarrel about it and she rushes off to the car. He goes with her, they drive off angrily, and both are killed when their car goes out of control. For many years of his long life, Joseph (as well as the other parents) finds himself thinking about how it all might have been different if he hadn't been so inflexible in rejecting his son and his bride.

So you must keep in mind the essential fact that your child is always your child, and question those rigidities embedded in you long ago so they do not unthinkingly interfere with the caretaking trust that has been granted to you by virtue of your parenthood.

I made a nice home for my husband and my children. Family came first. So it hurts me to see my son's wife just not taking good care of him. She's all involved in her career—she's chief probation officer for our county. She took a month off when she had a baby and now leaves the child all day with a hired woman. And my son does as much of the cooking and cleaning and shopping as she does. I think it's bad for my son and the baby. I try not to say anything but sometimes I can't help it. To me, that's not right.

* Belva Plain, *Evergreen.*

The increased number of women who establish careers and who see marriage in terms of an equal sharing of the household tasks has brought great changes in the marital "contract" and in child rearing. Like the woman above, many parents are so upset about arrangements that are greatly different from those they themselves had and from what they were taught was right that those arrangements seem unnatural. Yet these changes may make perfect sense to your child and his spouse, and he may be quite happy with them. Times have changed; new ways of running a marriage or a family have arisen out of these changes and may be perfectly appropriate to your children's needs and goals. So here it is best for you to stay out of it unless your views are asked for. Much trouble can be caused by comments such as, "You mean *you* take the clothes to the laundromat?" or "Doesn't it bother you that you don't have a meal on the table when he comes home from work?" or "How can you leave the baby all day with strangers?" You may not like it, but it really is their business and may work better for them than would your ideas.

Both my son and daughter are divorced. She was married twelve years and he was married four years. Now, why is that? My husband is one of four children and I'm one of three and not one divorce. Not one! But among all of our children—ours and our nieces and nephews—there are already six divorces. It's like an epidemic, and knowing that it's going around doesn't keep me from feeling very torn up about my own children. They run into a little trouble and they quit.

There's no secret about the rising divorce rate. These days, when couples celebrate a twenty-fifth anniversary, or even a tenth, it is a rare achievement. But while divorce may be more commonplace, when it happens to your children it can feel catastrophic. I know of parents of divorcing children who couldn't sleep for weeks, who intervened clumsily in the marital conflict in an attempt to prevent the split, and who attacked their children abusively.

There are many reasons why parents may react so strongly. They may be hurting for their own child. They may feel they can see even more clearly than their child the hard road ahead if he goes through with the divorce. They may be concerned that their son or daughter, whom they thought settled in a stable course in life, has suddenly become someone to worry about again. They may feel that he is being too impulsive and hasty, too unrealistic in his expectations of marriage. They may be deeply worried about the effects of the divorce on their grandchildren, if any. They may be ashamed of the divorce, feeling as if the divorce is somehow their failure. (This is particularly true if the parents have been competitive with others about their children and have been in the habit of letting others know how wonderful and *happy* their children are.)

All of these powerful feelings may bring the parents' own upset inner child to the surface. They may criticize and lecture and yell and berate. They may in essence say, "How can you do this to us?" (as if their children would take such a devastating step just to hurt their parents). They may make unwanted efforts to force the two partners to come together. In short, upset that their script as to how life was to go for their son or daughter has been ripped up, their inner child will often lash about in pain and protest. And what the parents may then lose sight of is that the primary casualties of the conflict are the divorcing parties themselves. At a time when their child is most devastated, traumatized, bereaved and frightened, they may be adding to the upset instead of providing the support and emotional nurturance their child may desperately need from them.

If there is ever a time when parents must control their own inner child reactions of criticizing and attacking, it is in responding to a child whose marriage is on the rocks. Because the inner child of your own son or daughter is understandably brought to the surface by the hurts and fears of his most important dream having been smashed, he will need you as a bulwark, as someone he can turn to for succor and sustenance, for advice and warmth in his tribulation. Even when it is your child who has initiated the divorce and who strongly wants it, there is much pain and upset for him. This does not mean that you hold back on your counsel and suggestions, which may include your insights on why they are making a mistake and how you feel the difficulties may be reconciled. But it must be with the understanding that it is their lives. They have had the unspoken experiences that have brought them to this point, and they will have to live with the consequences. And above all, it must be with the understanding that at a time like this, a "fella needs a friend" and a child needs a parent —not someone who adds to their distress but someone who is a rock and a comfort to the hurt little boy or girl in your grown-up son or daughter.

> *It was bad enough to adjust to the news that my daughter was getting a divorce. But when she told me that she's letting her husband have custody of their two children, I almost had a stroke! I'll never forgive her and I hardly have anything to do with her. Anyway, it's my son-in-law I have to keep a good relationship with if I want to see my grandchildren.*

Just a decade ago it was unthinkable that a divorcing woman would give up custody of her children to her husband. If a marriage ended, custody went to the mother as a natural right. Unless the mother was unfit, it was rarely challenged, and challenges were rarely successful. But the situation has changed. It is still by far the most common arrangement for mothers to assume responsibility for the rearing of the children after separation or divorce, but as part of the fallout of the explosive changes in male-female relationships (questioning of the old division of labor, women's interest in independence and careers, men's "domestication"), more and more fathers are receiving custody of their children. Not only are the courts now looking more favorably, or at least with less prejudice, on this possibility, but more women are agreeing, at times even insisting, that the father take the children. Here are some quotes from such mothers:

> I know women are supposed to want to hold on to their children no matter what, but I just don't feel that way. Harry will do a good job. He loves the kids and is very warm with them. And I want something different from my life now . . . my job is beginning to involve a lot of travel. . . .

> I wanted to end the marriage, my husband desperately didn't. He's very attached to me. It just didn't seem right that not only do I take myself from him, but that I take the

kids away, too. How much of a man's dream can you destroy?

I'm in love with someone else and I know we'll be married soon. I want to start from scratch. I'm sure I'll see the kids often. I love them, but so does their father. Besides, I centered my life around them for years—let him have a turn at it.

These statements reflect the main reasons women give for granting custody to their husbands. And husbands who ask for or fight for custody cite feelings that the children are theirs, too; that they have been close and nurturing with their children, maybe more so than their wives; that they will be able to provide at least as good if not a better home.*

If you are the parent of a woman giving up custody, you are likely to be much more upset than if you are the parent of a man receiving it. You may feel that your daughter is selfish and unnatural, and you may be afraid of losing access to your grandchild. (The latter fear is also there when a husband legally fights for and attains custody, and is a fear that the parents of a father have when the mother assumes custody, as is usually the case.) Again, your distress is understandable, but we can usually assume that your daughter has reasons for her decision in her understanding of her needs, her capacities and the total situation. It can be useful for you to advise that she take time with this decision so that it is not made impulsively out of fear, guilt, insecurity or a heady embrace of a new freedom. But beyond counseling a cautious pace, you will have to accept that the decision must be arrived at by the couple and that all involved will be suffering

* There is now a trend toward joint custody with both parents assuming equal responsibility for the children. This may or may not involve splitting the child's time—his living with one parent and then the other. How well joint custody can work and for whom it is advisable is not yet clear, but it seems to me the important thing is that *at least one parent* love the child enough to assume the caretaking role. What is to be feared is if neither parent wants custody, a tragic situation for the child and one in which the grandparents may be called on to step in. While this is rare, I hope the trend toward "doing your own thing" does not increase this sad irresponsibility.

pain: the pain of the parent who no longer will share the intimacy of the day-to-day living with the child; the pain of the parent who will undertake the burden of raising the child mostly alone; the pain of the child whose world has been broken and now has to adjust to a strange, new situation. It is important that your presence in the situation be a healing one, a balm for all rather than an abrasive one. How you react can make a big difference as to how smoothly or destructively the new arrangement goes. If you can respond from your most mature parental self rather than with the upset expectations of your distressed inner child, you will be a godsend to your children and your grandchildren. And in this role you are much more likely to keep your access to your grandchildren open than if you aggravate the situation or choose sides.

UNCONVENTIONAL LIFE-STYLES

My son was the sort of good boy who did everything he was supposed to. He played the cello, he played football, he shone glory on his parents. He never did anything bad. The only bad thing he did—he didn't do his homework, but even that was sort of amusing because you could say to yourself and to your husband, He's so bright he doesn't have to do his homework. . . . I come home from his college graduation and I find my good little boy has no job, no thoughts of a job, he is going to go wandering. Well, let me tell you, it was some experience for me. I had an anxiety attack, it was that severe a thing. . . . We pleaded with him. His father literally cried, I begged. He was calm about it, and said, "I'm sorry" and off he went.

The changes of the last two decades have not been limited to one or two areas, like sex and marriage, but have cut across the board, so much so that whole new phrases were born, like "counterculture" and "alternative life-styles." And one of the most striking changes that grew out of the social revolution of the sixties was a shift in, almost a reversal of, traditional attitudes toward work and achievement. Many of the parents of today's young adults had experienced the Depression and had come to value hard work that led to financial security and increasing material comfort. To "make a good living," to "be successful," to "provide well for your family" were unquestioned goals, and those who achieved them could be looked up to and could feel good about themselves and their accomplishments.

Many young people accepted the same goals as their parents, but others, never having known their parents' experiences of deprivation and insecurity, having had the leisure to question traditional values, and having been raised in an anti-establishment *zeitgeist*, rejected these objectives. Even small children approached school differently than had their parents. Whereas the parents of many of them had striven for good grades, for the approval of teachers, for the excitement of learning, many of these children took an attitude that can best be characterized as *anti-achievement*: They assumed a stance that was opposed to school work, antagonistic to the authority of the school, scornful toward the importance of education. Many dropped out far short of the educational goals their parents had for them. You could hear similar refrains over and over from young people:

> "Why knock myself out? The courses are irrelevant and grades are meaningless."
>
> "You'll never get me in a nine-to-five job."
>
> "I'm not going to be like you, working and buying and spending most of it on us kids. What's that all about? When did you have fun? When did you live for yourself?"

(The last can be particularly infuriating to the parents, who hadn't noticed that the kids were opposed to their spending all that time and money on them before.)

The pendulum is swinging back, as pendulums do, so that youth again are interested in accomplishing and attaining, but it has not gone back to where it was, and many parents find themselves perplexed by their children's feelings about work and money. Often a child's unwillingness to accept the structure and demands of certain work and educational settings puts him at odds with parents who have valued responsibility and excellence.

There have also been changes of a very different kind in attitudes toward work: the wider range of occupational alternatives for women. Even though themselves reared at a time when a woman, if she worked at all, was expected to be a clerical worker, a retail store salesgirl, a nurse or schoolteacher while she waited for a husband, many parents have now accepted the idea of other new career possibilities for their daughters. But others still see a woman's decision to have a career as a dangerous straying from accepted roles and values and therefore are very upset when their daughter makes this choice. I have written at length elsewhere * about the relationship between Karen and her mother. Karen's parents disapproved of extended education for her and didn't come to her college graduation. For a long time, Karen avoided telling them that she planned to go to law school. Finally, when she was accepted by the school, she told her mother about it in a burst of enthusiasm and excitement. Her mother was stunned.

"Have you gone mad?"

"There's nothing crazy about being a lawyer."

"We'll never have any grandchildren from you."

"What has that got to do with it? They don't tie my tubes when I pass the bar exam."

"Karen, you mustn't use language like that. I have tried to teach you that there are things good women do and things they don't do. Good women are not men."

It was hard for this mother to accept her daughter's role for a long time. Karen's steadfastness forced her mother to confront her own values and to see that times change, new options appear, and values must have some flexibility. How much flexibility, each parent must decide for himself, but for this and other categories of disappointed expectations we will discuss, there is one factor we must come to terms with in ourselves. We must realize that our parents trained us in accordance with the expectations of their time and place. We will tend to expect behavior from our children in terms of our own time and place. But if the rules and expectations that were quite appropriate for our generation are out-of-step with our children's generation, then insisting on that behavior from them can be an invitation to conflict.†

* Howard Halpern, *Cutting Loose*, p. 117.

† We will see later that parents cannot and should not be completely flexible, cannot and should not set aside all their beliefs about what is or is not acceptable behavior from their children.

What you decide to do if your son or daughter has an approach to schooling or work that is anathema to you and your expectations will depend a lot on what you *can* do. If your child is dependent on you financially and therefore using your money to back a course you disapprove of, you will have more leverage than if he is not. For example, suppose you are paying for his college and he's just putting in time there, attending few classes, rarely completing his assignments, and failing or nearly failing many of his courses. Let us assume that you have tried to help him remedy the situation by discussing the matter thoroughly, listening to his explanations as to what is wrong, offering your advice, suggesting that he avail himself of the college counseling service, etc. But he continues to put minimal effort into school, shows little interest in any academic area, and continues to get poor grades. *At a certain point a parent is entitled to say, "I'm not going to shell out any more money for this."*

The appropriate point for parents to use their financial leverage to influence a child's life is not always clear and will depend on the parents' judgment as to the meaning of their child's behavior. If they see it as laziness and irresponsibility, they will probably respond differently than if they see it as reflecting a more serious problem. I remember a young man who, after getting very high grades his first year as a premedical student, went on a sleeping binge during his second year, with the result that he failed four out of five courses. His father, a doctor, was disappointed and angry that his son had made acceptance into medical school an impossibility by this debacle. His first reaction was to threaten that he would not pay further for college. But as they discussed it, what emerged was that the son didn't really want to be the physician he was always expected to be. It had been assumed he would be a doctor for so many years that this young man did not realize he didn't wish to be a doctor until he fell into a depression (manifested by the sleeping binge), and the resulting sabotage of his medical school possibilities forced him to confront a long-buried wish to be a writer (Creative Writing was the one course he did not fail). His parents backed him in a switch to the School of Journalism. His grades went up again, and by his senior year he was editor of the college newspaper. Before he was thirty he was a syndicated columnist and had a growing reputation for his powerful use of words.

Undeniably you have the right to use an economic veto with a grown-up child who is still financially dependent on you, and in many instances it is the most appropriate and helpful action to take. But as we have just seen, it may not be the wisest thing to do. Understanding your son or daughter may put you in touch with meanings of his behavior that you hadn't suspected. You may see that his current attitudes toward school or work are a passing but important stage in establishing a sense of identity. Or you may find that his approach, though so different from yours, has a value and validity of its own, and your resistance to it is based on ideas and expectations that might well need some reappraisal. So before you pull the financial plug, make sure you've explored the complexities of his motivation and your own.

Counterculture

Not all the newer approaches to living and earning a living involve simply a different attitude toward work but combine with the newer attitudes toward sex, relationships and values to form whole new "countercultural" modes. Take this excerpt from a father speaking during an informal conversation among a few parents of grown-up children at a resort hotel.

My daughter is living in what I can only call a commune, although she doesn't call it that. She and seven others have a house about sixty miles out of the city where they share everything together. There are currently three men and five women, although that changes. I'm not sure what the sexual arrangements are, the relationships seem shifting. . . . I wouldn't have minded it too much if she were nineteen but she's twenty-nine, and she's been living there for two years, eating organic food, weaving small rugs which she sells to a local craft shop. . . . There's no thought of marriage, of children, of what I would call a future.

A mother in the group added, "It's almost the same thing with my son. He's twenty-six and for the past two years he has been living at this Yoga Ashram, studying with his guru. I must say it's peaceful there, and he looks very serene in his white robe or whatever you call it. He's very soft-spoken now and won't get into any arguments with me, but I feel he's a stranger. He's not the boy I know. If I think of him still there in ten years or twenty years I feel sick. What kind of a phony excuse for life is that?"

Many parents are concerned about the newer and more organized countercultural movements, such as communes, all-embracing political movements, and powerful religious evangelical groups. Christians have been threatened by Eastern gurus and their mysticism; Jews have been threatened by proselytizing groups, such as Jews for Jesus; both have been threatened by religious totalitarian movements, such as the Moonies. The threat comes from the strong impact such groups have on some of their children, taking them not only in new and strange directions, but at times directly interfering with the maintenance of almost any meaningful relationship with their parents.

If your child is pursuing a life that is so different, in some essential ways, from what you envisioned that you are very unhappy about it, or get into frequent conflict with him about it, here are some questions you must ask yourself:

—Is he old enough to make this choice?

—Does he seem happy with it?

—Does it seem to be meeting his needs?

—Is it seriously harmful to himself or others?

—Is he being unduly influenced in this choice?

—Is your antagonism because you really see it's having destructive effects or because your inner child, which is as upset by change as are all little children (did you ever try to read a tot a bedtime story he is familiar with and leave out a word?), is upset by the unexpected and unfamiliar?

If your child is legally of age to make major decisions about the direction of his life and if he is content with his decisions, you will probably have to stop *active* opposition to your child's choices if you are not to do damage to the relationship. But you can certainly let him know how you feel and can present your reasons for opposing the choices he has made as persuasively as you are able. (Only if he is being influenced by brainwashing techniques, by being held incommunicado or by the flagrant abuse of drugs would strong and special interventions be called for.)

Beyond the Pale

It is hard to raise a child without having dreams and expectations, and it is desolating to see those expectations violated. But in most instances, it is wisdom to accept the reality of your child's life and come to terms with his right to follow a path that is different from the one you would have wished him to pursue. This can be particularly difficult when his path is one you find not just strange, but repugnant, and you will need to assuage and control the distressed child inside yourself so that a more mature perspective may prevail.

If you believe that your child is headed in a destructive direction, there are two possible outcomes—either you will be wrong or you will be right. If you are wrong, it means your child's chosen path is a good one for him, which should please you. And if you are right, if he has made a choice that is truly dangerous and misguided, he will need the relationship with you more than ever. Either way, it is almost always best not to react in ways that will destroy your availability. And your being there for him when he is traveling a hard road can create a very gratifying bond of caring.

Occasionally, however, a child may choose a path that leads so far beyond what you can accept—a way of life that is so abhorrent, so against everything you believe in, and that so permeates his interactions with you—that you cannot be receptive to him or his path. *It may then be necessary to reduce or even discontinue your ties with him* (as did Tevye when Chava's marital choice violated his whole belief system). Everyone has the right to place limits on what behavior he will tolerate in his relationship with another person, no matter who that person is. You have a right to state, in essence: "We are two different individuals. I care about you, but I don't need an ongoing relationship with you so badly that I will pay any price. I do not need you to validate me. I wish the way you choose to live is one I could appreciate and enjoy, but it is actually so far beyond the pale of what I find acceptable that I will stop pursuing an active relationship with you as long as this situation exists. I do this not as a punishment, not as a coercion, but out of my own self-respect."

This is one of the most solemn steps a parent can take, one that can have profound and irrevocable consequences. So it should never be taken until you have tried very hard to suspend judgment, to grasp fully that your child is an independent person and not an extension of your expectations, and to increase your flexibility in what you can accept. But if this step must be taken, it can be liberating for you both to stop living in the constant tension of irreconcilable differences and to recognize that even parents and their progeny are ultimately separate beings.

CHAPTER 8

Sunrise, Sunset

Interspersed among her humorous pieces, Erma Bombeck has written a few essays that evoke a powerful sense of the passage of time in the parent-child relationship. In one she recounts how, from the time Mike was a toddler, his father was always concerned that Mike's activities would kill the grass. Whether it was the sandbox he wanted at three, the jungle gym and swings at five, the plastic swimming pool, the tent-outs, the basketball hoop, his father complained about the damage being done to the lawn. Each time he expressed worry about the grass, his wife would smile and say, "It'll come back." Bombeck ends her piece like this:

> The lawn this fall was beautiful. It was green and alive and rolled out like a sponge carpet along the drive where gym shoes had trod . . . along the garage where bicycles used to fall . . . and around the flower beds where little boys used to dig with iced tea spoons.

But Mike's father never saw it. He anxiously looked beyond the yard and asked with a catch in his voice, "He will come back, won't he?" *

Our children grow older, and as they do, their lives enter different stages and achieve new landmarks. And as our children get older, so do we, and we enter new stages not just because of our advancing years, but because some of the developmental steps our children take are landmarks in our own lives. When they get married or when they have children, our feelings about ourselves, our outlook on life, our sense of identity and our relationship with them may profoundly change. Yet, through all the changes in them and in us, we remain their parents. We will be looking at two developmental "passages" that we, as parents of adults, go through because of the changes our children make in their own lives. We will look at what happens when our children make us parents-in-law † and when they make us grandparents.

Becoming a Parent-in-Law

Few actions your children might take are as likely to arouse such a mixture of emotions in you as his or her getting married. There may be great joy (particularly if you are happy about the person chosen); there can be choking sentiment ("Is this the little girl I carried? Is this the little boy at play?"); there can be grief at losing your place as the most important source of emotional supplies in your child's life; and there can be a sense of emptiness at the loss of a role that has been part of your basic identity for so many years. Therese Benedek put it this way:

* Erma Bombeck, *If Life Is a Bowl of Cherries*, p. 191.

† Increasingly, young people are becoming couples without being "in-laws" simply by living together without laws. Many of the issues are the same as those that will be discussed here. But for a discussion of some of the issues you may face when your children live with someone to whom they are not married, see Chapter 7.

> With a child's marriage, the immediate responsibility of parenthood for that child is discontinued. The parents cease to be the closest of kin by law, since the new husband and wife, even if they have known each other for only a few weeks or months, have become the next of kin. Their own parents, having lived with them through the early and middle phases of parenthood, enter a new, last phase of parenthood. They are not, however, old people yet. . . . *

Such awareness of change and feelings of loss are as natural as your tears at the wedding, but if these feelings persist over a long period of time and if they lead you to act possessively with your child, competitively with your son-in-law or daughter-in-law, or intrusively with the couple, there is one thing we can be sure of: *Your inner child is acting up and trying desperately to avert feelings of being rejected and abandoned.* And we can predict that as long as your actions are dominated by that child within you, you are likely to behave in ways that may be destructive to your offspring, to his marriage, and to your relationship with the new couple. For when your son or daughter marries, you are confronted with having to make a shift within yourself that requires your rising to new heights of parental maturity. Actually, it is a double shift. It means seeing your child in this new light, with his primary relationship no longer with you, and it means accepting his spouse fully into the family. "The parents have a new developmental task to accomplish; they have to encompass the husband of their daughter or the wife of their son, not only in their own family but also in their own psychic systems as an object of their love. . . . But the . . . relationship to the in-law remains shaky for some time." †

The difficult step demanded of you is the acceptance of a new couple, a new nuclear family, in which your child and spouse have chosen each other for a myriad of complex emotional reasons and chemical attractions that you could not possibly know,

* In *Parenthood,* edited by E. J. Anthony and Therese Benedek (Boston: Little Brown, 1970), Chapter 8, "Parenthood During the Life Cycle," p. 196.

† *Ibid.*, p. 196.

and whose couplehood has a validity and commitment as great as those you have had with the members of the family you grew up in or you created. You have known your child long and loved him deeply, but your child's spouse will know facets of him that are profound and beyond your imagining, and will love your child in ways that are the same and yet enormously different from your loving. They must plan and create a life together, based on their mutual needs and goals. Their plan may be similar to your expectations of it, or quite different, but it is their script to write and to live. Being a couple is a difficult task, and their endeavor will be so much easier if they have the gift of your benign loving.

But here you must be brutally honest with yourself. It can feel like loving concern to give advice on everything from where and how they should live, how they should furnish, where they should buy, when they should have children, and how they should be with each other. And it may indeed be loving concern if such advice is requested by them. But unbidden intervention like this stems from your inner child who can't let go, who can't let your son or daughter establish a life apart from you. And it can stem from the little child inside yourself who strongly identifies with your son or daughter, seeing him as an extension of you. In this identification, you may rush to be on your offspring's side just as you used to when he was beset by the neighborhood bully or a destructive teacher. But this time the adversary you see as threatening your child's happiness is his spouse, whether there is good reason for you to believe this or not.* Your long habit of protectiveness and of seeing your child as part of yourself can lead you to lay blame on the other rather than your own child. (Other parents, with a history of being very critical of their own offspring, may automatically blame their own child if he is having conflict with his spouse. This also arises from the inner child of the parents whose own parents may have been into a blaming Song and Dance with them.)

So, taking the unrequested role of advice-giver, counselor, bargain hunter, arbitrator or attention demander is not what I

* At times, your adversary may seem to be not your child-in-law, but his parents, and your inner child may enter into a rivalry with them for your child's affections, perhaps repeating an old sibling rivalry.

mean when I say that your married children would gain much from your benign loving. I mean they would gain much if you communicated a caring concern with the success of their marriage enterprise and their finding happiness in it. Your benign loving means being attuned to their messages as to how you can be most helpful to them rather than your deciding how they ought to be helped by you. It means accepting your child's spouse as his primary commitment and showing that it is fine with you.

This can be a difficult stance to take. The little child in you may scream in anger and sadness at the loss of the old type of tie. That is why I say it will require the highest exercise of your parental maturity. But if you exercise it, you can enter into a new kind of relationship with your child and maybe with your son-in-law or daughter-in-law that is much more gratifying and appropriate than the old interaction.

Your Married Daughter

One of the most complex emotional entanglements exists between a mother and her married daughter. Here is her girl, this same-sexed flesh of her flesh, this semiclone who shares a similar body and similar physiology and has been reared with many of the same social expectations that she, the mother, has known. She is the carrier of many of her mother's unfinished dreams. And now, in becoming a wife, this daughter has assumed a role that makes her more similar to her mother, yet takes her further away. So it comes as no source of wonderment that at the time when mothers most should let go, they often find new ways of trying to hold on. Let's look again at the insights of Therese Benedek.

> Instead of consciously attempting to relax their influence upon their daughters, mothers unconsciously identify with them and want to be involved in every detail of their new life. Frequent visits to their daughter's household, meant to be helpful, often become like an inspection that enrages the daughter and irritates her husband. It can go even farther, becoming a kind of inquisition regarding her life with her husband, his work, his income, etc., which enrages the

son-in-law and in turn makes the mother-in-law an unwelcome visitor. . . .*

What makes such a mother's understandable identification with her daughter get so out of hand that it overrules the parental wisdom which would tell her that her daughter needs more space? It is the mother's inner child who is afraid of the abandonment she anticipates in the daughter's marital commitment. So this well-meaning mother can become the disliked and ridiculed mother-in-law of the old "mother-in-law jokes" of a decade or two ago, before daughters claimed their separations more clearly and therefore spared their husbands from too much mother-in-law intrusion. If you are accused of being one of those interfering caricatures, you owe it to yourself and your child to listen and evaluate the couple's complaint, to recognize the little girl in yourself who is trying to hold on to this old sense of closeness and identity, and then to relinquish your daughter to her new life partner as her basic relationship.

Fathers have other problems when their daughters marry. They can be outright jealous. They have raised their darling daughters and gone through all the hardships and expenses and now, when she is most ripe and lovely, someone else carries her off. And this someone is usually a good deal younger than the father, with more energy, fewer aches and wrinkles, and greater real or fancied virility. But it is hard for fathers to acknowledge this jealousy. It often hides behind his focus on the young man's inadequacies and his fatherly concern that his son-in-law take care of his daughter and be as good to her as he was. If you are the father of a married daughter, it may take some adjusting to accept her husband as the number one man in her life. You will have to deal with that jealous and possessive little boy in you who wants center stage all to himself, so you can take an appropriate paternal role of giving the symbolic blessing that is inherent in your respect for their couplehood.

As father, you may often find yourself in the job of peacemaker between mother and daughter or mother and son-in-law because the profound tie that exists between mother and daughter may

* Anthony and Benedek, *Parenthood*, p. 197.

make mother's intense reactions to the daughter's marriage more long-lasting than your own, and therefore, you may be able to step back, see the conflicts in greater perspective, and try to negotiate. This can be a difficult but very useful role. To succeed at it, you will have to recognize the feelings of all parties: those of your wife, whose needs to hold on may be accentuated if she is depressed or is entering menopause; those of your daughter, who may be in conflict between her desire to center her life around her marriage and her old, deep ties to her mother; and those of your son-in-law, who married your daughter and not her parents and who wants a chance to build a marriage based on the needs and desires of the two of them. If you can negotiate successfully, much tension can be allayed. If you cannot, either because the parties will not let you or because of your own possessive inner child, then the chances are you will feel you have to stand by and protect your wife. But every effort should be made to remain caringly available to all involved.

Your Married Son

A mother may often feel that she is losing her son in a marriage ("A son is a son till he takes him a wife"). She hopes that at least her daughter-in-law will make him a fine home and take care of him as well as she did. This makes it all too easy for the competitive little girl in mother to become critical of her son's wife, and this is likely to arouse angry and rebellious feelings in the daughter-in-law. The son can be unhappily caught in the middle. You can avoid this kind of agonizing ongoing conflict by setting aside the competitive child in yourself and by resolving *never* to tell your daughter-in-law what your son likes, how to cook his food, how to decorate his house, etc., unless you are clearly and *explicitly* asked. Your son has chosen this woman and she has chosen him, and they will have to learn how to please each other.

A father may feel that his son, in marrying, has stepped into the arena with him as a rival male. He may see his son as having chosen a pretty young woman (no matter what her appearance, she will have the beauty of youth in the eyes of the father); he may see his son at the hopeful beginning of a road he, the father, has long traveled. Sometimes additional competitive factors enter, as when the son has a profession with more status than the father, or makes more money, or enters the father's business. If you become aware of such feelings of rivalry with your son, this awareness in itself will probably keep you from acting on them destructively, but if you still react competitively, you must explore further, looking into whether current dissatisfactions with your own marriage or with other aspects of your life are coloring the picture, and whether the rivalrous and demanding little boy from your past has emerged to take control of your actions. Your son will still want you as a source of support, a model of strength and a friendly mentor, and you will have to bring the mature parenting part of yourself to the fore if you are to give him, your daughter-in-law and yourself the rich gratifications of this role.

Your Child's Spouse as Adversary

As difficult as it may be lovingly to encompass your child's couplehood when you like her spouse, it is many times more difficult when you don't like him, or see him as abusive to your child, or feel he dislikes you, or feel he is trying to turn your child against you. And all of these things are possible. You may have reason to dislike your child's choice of mate. Perhaps you see him as selfish, or irresponsible, or a loser. You may see evidence that he treats your offspring cruelly or insensitively or exploitively. His dislike of you can be unmistakable at times, and he may be trying to get your child to shut you out of their lives. But you must first check out such possibilities to be sure that they are not the distortions of your possessive and angry inner child, an inner child who may have turned your child's spouse into a hated sibling rival of the past, or an inner child who is unwilling to share attentions with anyone.

If you have checked out the possibilities that you are distorting and are still convinced that your son-in-law or daughter-in-law is a person who earns your dislike, it is even more important to be the wisest and most mature parent you can be if you are not to damage, perhaps irreparably, your relationship with your child. But dealing with the situation with wisdom can test your restraint to the breaking point when the provocation is great. Here are three vignettes of extremely frustrating situations between parents and their married children.

Mrs. Lewis knew that her daughter-in-law Greta despised her. She had sensed it very early in the relationship, long before her son Victor married her. Greta's manner was curt and cool with both Mr. and Mrs. Lewis. At times she was openly hostile. Mr. and Mrs. Lewis tried to make the interaction warmer and closer, but it only got worse. It was almost impossible to arrange to spend time with Victor and his wife. Mrs. Lewis called her daughter-in-law and confronted Greta with her feeling that Greta didn't like her. After a few attempts at avoidance, Greta said, "You're right. You come on so gushy and bubbly I think you're a phony. And besides, my philosophy is that children should separate completely from parents if they are to grow up. I think that what you want is to keep Victor a baby. Why don't you just leave us alone?"

(We will return later to see what happened in this tense situation. But first let's look at other examples.)

Mr. and Mrs. Friend were delighted with their new son-in-law Gerd. He was a young accountant who seemed to have lots of self-confidence and ambition, and he had courted their daughter Jill attentively. There was minor conflict when Gerd opposed the wishes of Jill and her parents to have a large wedding, hinting that he would rather the parents give them the money it cost, but then he went along with the wedding plans. Soon after, Gerd made it clear to his father-in-law, who headed a chain of furniture stores, that he expected the company's accounting work to go to him. Mr. Friend explained that his current accountant had been a close boyhood chum who had been the first and only accountant the business had known, who had contributed to its success, and whom he couldn't possibly replace. He did promise to try to get Gerd work from other businessmen he knew and to bring him into the picture when his old friend phased out or retired. Gerd was furious. He began to tell his wife that her parents were selfish, cheap, didn't like him and didn't care about her. An open conflict developed between Gerd and his in-laws with Jill torn between them. She began increasingly to take Gerd's side.

(We'll also be back to the Friends and their unhappy relationship with this young couple. But one last illustrative vignette.)

From the first moment Mr. Heller met Arnold, a freelance photographer, he felt Arnold was a self-centered opportunist. He had come to pick Sunny up on what was only their second date, and the next morning Mr. Heller told his daughter, "I don't like that guy. He's too slick and there's nothing warm about him. He's like a reptile." Sunny was resentful, and whether her continuing to see Arnold was rebellion or she was genuinely attracted to him will never be known, but in less than a year they were married and her parents welcomed Arnold into the family. A year later they had a child, but at about this time Arnold let Sunny know that he had a deteriorative muscular disease which would increasingly paralyze him. And he had known about it long before their marriage but had never told Sunny! Sunny was beset by a torrent of conflicting feelings: anger at being deceived, concern about Arnold, worry about the future, feelings of being trapped, guilt about wanting out, etc. It took a while before she had the courage to share this development with her parents.

While the marriage of our children usually does not lead to situations as laden with unpleasantness between the new couple and ourselves as these three examples, they are by no means uncommon. We have probably all heard parents say, "We always got along so well until he got married." Perhaps you have heard yourselves say it. Let's take a closer look at these three troubled families to discover what went on and how each has turned out up until this time.

When Greta told her mother-in-law that she disliked her and believed Mrs. Lewis only wanted a continued relationship with them to keep Victor a baby, Mrs. Lewis was swept with outrage and dismay. She wanted to start screaming at Greta, but she said, "Greta, I'm sorry you don't like me but that's your privilege. But you're very wrong about my wanting to keep Victor a baby. I love him and intend to keep having a relationship with him." And she quickly got off the phone. She talked it over with her husband and they decided on their position. Mr. Lewis dropped into his son's office the next day, told him what Greta had said to Mrs. Lewis and then said, "Mother and I want you to know that we're sorry Greta feels the way she does. We don't want to interfere between you, but neither do we intend to cave in to her interference in your relationship with us. You're entitled to a relationship with us without having to make a choice between her and us, and I hope you'll find a way of handling it that doesn't harm what you have with us or Greta."

Victor made it very clear to Greta that he loved his parents and intended to maintain a relationship with them. Greta called him a "mama's boy" and refused to accompany him when he would visit, but he persisted. He tried to accommodate his wife by seeing his parents less frequently than before, by calling them from his office and not from home, but he persisted in having reasonable contact with them. Greta's rage turned against Victor more and more viciously. She would accuse him of doing things only because his parents told him to when this was far from the truth. One night she was haranguing him about it until nearly dawn while he begged her to let him get some sleep. She suddenly jumped up and said, "If you want them so much, then go back to them. I'm finished." She packed a bag, left, and the marriage was over except for the legal formalities.

Months later his parents told him they could not get over a nagging sense of guilt that if they had bowed out of the picture, his marriage would not have broken up. Victor said, "But I didn't want you out of the picture. Besides, it had to end sooner or later. Greta was a possessive, selfish little girl who tried to cut off all my relationships with the outside world. She was the one who was too tied to her parents. She called them a couple of times every day but would start slamming doors and drawers when I spoke to you on the phone. And she's back living with them now."

When a person unjustifiably tries to turn his spouse against his spouse's own parents, he often may be very closely bound to his own parents. Like Greta, he may accuse his mate of being too involved with his parents and may say terrible things about his parents while not being aware that he himself is overly involved with his own parents. What is happening is that the little girl or boy in this son-in-law or daughter-in-law does not want to make a healthy separation from his own parents, wants to include his spouse completely in the orbit of his own parents, and sees the spouse's parental relationship as a threat to this endeavor. In addition, it is often true that the secret hostile and angry feelings toward his own parents cannot be allowed into awareness but are acted out instead against the spouse's parents. (A further complication is sometimes present when this grown-up child really likes his in-laws, perhaps even unconsciously preferring them to his own parents, and reacts against this threatening feeling by making his in-laws into devils.)

Sometimes the reason for this kind of unjustified vendetta against in-laws is different. The inner child of the angry son-in-law or daughter-in-law may still be so caught up in his own rebellion (an unresolved "You Bother Me Too Much" attempt at defiant separateness) that he is at war with all parents (and perhaps all authorities) including his own as well as his mate's. If you are the target of this, you know how frustrating it can be.

The stance of Mr. and Mrs. Lewis provides a helpful guide to handling this kind of conflict. They did not get into an angry battle with their son or daughter-in-law, a reaction that would have stemmed largely from their own inner child and would have led to an interminable Song and Dance. They managed to call on the mature parenting part of themselves, simply telling Greta they felt she saw it wrong and telling Victor they did not want to cause him to choose between Greta and them but felt that he and they were entitled to continue a caring, sensible, nonintrusive relationship. The more they and Victor reacted as adults, the more the demanding inner child of Greta emerged and, unfortunately, Greta was not able to shift enough to maintain the marital relationship.

The ending was quite different for the Friends, whose son-in-law Gerd became their enemy when Mr. Friend would not immediately turn over the accounting work of his corporation to him. Jill feared Gerd's brittle anger, and the little girl in Jill was so terrified of his leaving her that almost no price was too much to pay to avoid it. And the price the self-centered, greedy little boy in Gerd demanded was that Jill terminate her relationship with her parents. Jill was in great conflict over this but went along with Gerd. What enabled her to make this decision was not only her fears of Gerd's abandonment, but that so much of her unresolved little girl dependency feelings had simply switched from her parents to Gerd, so she didn't need them as much anymore. And her old anger at her parents, because there had been considerable early conflicts, made it easy for her to buy Gerd's charges against them. Her parents made many attempts to re-establish contact but were always rebuffed. Then Gerd took a position with a company half a continent away. That was the end of all communication except for exchanges of birthday cards and Christmas cards. It's been five years since this rupture, and both parents bear a resigned sadness. Mr. Friend told me, "I hear she's happy with him so I try to be content with that. I still feel that when they both get more mature they will come around." In truth, about all they can do is what they are doing: making it clear they would welcome a return to more of a relationship, but otherwise going on to enjoy the other aspects of their lives. They can continue to enjoy the reports that Jill seems happy, rather than let the pain and wishes for revenge of their own inner child lead them to feel cheated, left out and resentful of Jill's happiness. For in contrast, many a parent who is cut off from his child by the child's mate must also endure reports of his child's unhappiness.

Finally, there are Mr. and Mrs. Heller and their daughter Sunny. I've mentioned how Sunny was flooded with a turbulent mixture of emotions when she belatedly learned of her husband's deteriorative muscular illness. Well, her parents experienced a similar maelstrom of feelings, but the predominant one, at least at first, was fury at Arnold. "That selfish, lying bastard," Mr. Heller screamed. He wanted to rush over to their house and "make his death a lot quicker." Mrs. Heller made inquiries about an annulment because of the deception involved. Their understandable rage took over so completely that for a while they lost sight of Sunny and her needs and feelings in this predicament. I have known situations where parents act on their anger at their son-in-law or daughter-in-law and not only make the situation worse, but they place their own child in the middle and make it impossible for their child to turn to them for support. But the Hellers were able to deal with their anger well enough to bring the mature parenting part of themselves to the fore. They let Sunny know they would stand by her in whatever decisions she made, and in the meantime, they would try to be as much help to the two of them as they could. Mrs. Heller said, "It was hard not to say 'I told you so' but what was the point? I have no respect for him and Sunny certainly knows that, but she's got enough trouble without us on her back." And Mr. Heller said, "I can see where Arnold got to be the way he is. His mother thinks he's God Almighty and his father is a schemer, just like Arnold. I told Arnold I thought he was an S.O.B. for keeping his illness secret, but they both know they can count on us."

What is the best way for you to approach the problem of a son-in-law or daughter-in-law you dislike or think is bad for your child? The following examples point to a few simple guidelines.

1. Check out carefully whether your feelings are justified or are the products of your inner child rivalries or your disappointment that your child's choice does not live up to your dreams and expectations.
2. If your child is contemplating marriage to someone you feel you have good reason to be concerned about, share these concerns with your child directly and openly, without condemnation, threats or attack. Make it clear that you recognize it is his or her decision, and you have no wish to make this issue a cause for a rift in your loving relationship with him.
3. If your child chooses to marry despite your expressed negative feelings about the chosen person, give your child as much backing as you honestly can. Your child will certainly need that support if you are right about his choice. Avoid making your child feel he must choose between yourself and the intended mate. To the best of your ability, welcome the new member of the family.
4. Remember that once your child has made his choice, the person chosen is rightfully and most appropriately your child's prime commitment.
5. Bear in mind that people change, and young people grow up, and the person your child has married may be quite different in a few years. Hostile defiance on the part of your child and his spouse may fade as they find they have successfully established their independence.
6. Keep yourself focused on the primary task of maintaining a

caring relationship with your child (if he will let you), but be prepared to withdraw to a minimally involved distance (if he will not let you).

7. Keep in mind that your judgment of your child's spouse as a bad choice for him may be wrong. Your son or daughter will probably have a better idea of what kind of person meets his needs than you do. I've seen many marriages where the parents were in opposition and prophesied disaster, but the couple went on to be quite happy with their marriage and each other. So put aside what you would have wanted for your child and have some faith and trust in your child's judgment. Listen to the words of this father as he discusses his daughter's choice in a husband:

> We have one daughter, Eleanor. Her first serious guy was sort of the ideal son-in-law type. He adored her and she liked him very much. And it looked like they'd be married. He was manly and capable and the guy-around-the-house, and very solicitous and so forth. We were very excited about him, and yet, in the end, Eleanor found him too possessive. She took up with a Dartmouth chap who seemed to us interesting and smart but physically and emotionally less attractive than the first fellow she had. He's Swiss, very precise and, we always felt, a little stingy. He's the sort of fellow, we thought then, might carry a little purse and when he opened it a moth would fly out. We liked him all right but gee, not for her. But Eleanor said, "No, he understands me better and I like him better and I'm going with him now." So this is the guy she married. And from the original feeling of, Well, Eleanor likes him, Eleanor knows what she's doing, Eleanor's awfully smart, he doesn't seem to us as good as the first guy but Eleanor likes him, and so forth, we have come to think that she was dead right. This guy hangs it all over the other guy. He's very, very interesting and suits and satisfies her.

These parents, disappointed at first, were wise enough not to interfere. They respected their daughter's judgment and after a while came to agree with it. It doesn't always happen this way but often enough. In general, if you can embrace the couple and side with their difficult task of making an intimate relationship flourish, you can quietly share both the joys and the heartaches of that task.

Being a Grandparent

Most parents of married children sooner or later begin to experience a deep longing to have grandchildren. What prompts this yearning? It is probably a combination of many things.

- If you believe that raising children is an essential experience for personal fulfillment, then you will be eager to see your child begin that experience.
- In having grandchildren you can glimpse a kind of immortality. Even more clearly than when you had your own children, you can see yourself as a link in the human chain that stretches from the primeval horizon of the unknown past to the ever-receding horizon of the unknowable future. As a part of that chain, you will always exist.
- You may long to relive a relationship with a baby, to mobilize and utilize the part of yourself that is deeply caretaking and nurturing, for it is a part of yourself that may have lain fallow for many years because you have not been needed in that way.
- You may sense that now you can be that nurturing person much more fully than you may have been able to be when you had young children of your own, for now you are more mature, your life is no longer driven by the struggle to establish yourself or by the conflicts of the early stages of a marriage. And you do not have the stress of the responsibility for nursing, training, disciplining and providing for this child. You are free, therefore, to have one of the great joys in life, an unparalleled delight that few people experience often—the joy of unconditional, uncomplicated, unambivalent loving!

This unambivalent grandparental loving is a precious gift to the grandchild. "The love of the grandparents gives the child a sense of security in being loved without always deserving it. Thus the undemanding love of the grandparents preserves for the child a piece of the self-indulgent sense of omnipotence experienced unconsciously during infancy. What does the grandparent receive in return? A loving glance from a happy child, a trusting hand, an actual appeal for help, a warm, feverish body clinging—whatever it is, for better or for worse, it is a message conveyed to the grandparent that he or she is needed, wanted and loved, so they really feel like good parents, accepted gratefully by the child. This is the token of a new lease on life cherished by all."*

What a beautiful exchange of precious emotional gifts it can be! But often, as you may have discovered, being a grandparent does not develop as blissfully as that, because how it goes is largely a product of your relationship with your grandchild's parents. And that relationship may have a troubled history with conflicts that are compounded by the appearance of the grandchild. The couple has become a family with the greater purpose of sheltering and rearing a new generation. That demanding and fulfilling enterprise, while in some ways increasing your child's identification with you, in other ways increases his or her separateness from you. And at just the time you want so much to be part of it.

These differences in direction between you and your child and child-in-law need not prevent a harmonious relationship from developing between you, them, and your grandchild if your and your offspring's inner child can be kept from interfering. And chances are that if you keep your eye on your own inner child, that of your own son or daughter will become less and less an obstacle. So let's look at what you have to be aware of in yourself.

First, you need be aware that your understandable desire to be of help and to teach your son or daughter what you know of parenting skills can become, if ruled by your inner child, an unwelcome intrusion into the life of your son or daughter. Whether the issue be how and what the child is fed, or how and when he is toilet trained, or if he is dressed too warmly or not warmly enough, or how he should be disciplined or, in general, how the child is brought up, you must recognize that this whole area is his parents' rightful province, and you should assume that there is a

* Anthony and Benedek, *Parenthood*, p. 201.

big "Keep Out" sign there unless you are specifically invited in. If not, your "Let me do it" or "Do it this way" can run into, "I can do it myself. Leave me alone!" More than once, I have heard stories of grandparents who, when spending a day with their grandchild, had his hair cut when the parents had been very happy with the child's hair as it was! This is an insensitive usurpation of the parents' role and usually leads to rage on the part of these young parents and their limiting the child's visits with his grandparents. Everyone loses. If you tend to do things like this, try to recognize that such actions could not possibly arise out of your mature wisdom but from the little willful and impulsive child in you that wants his own way.

Second, you have to be aware that your wish to reach out to your grandchild and have that special relationship with him, if ruled by your inner child, can lead you to bypass and undercut the parents in ways that may be unwittingly disrespectful of the young couple and infuriating to them. For example, I know of grandparents who buy their grandchildren candy when the parents have explicitly asked them not to. "What harm can it do?" they may ask. "We see him only once a week." But it can do harm, perhaps to the child's teeth or metabolism, possibly to the child's feelings about his own parents, and almost certainly to the grandparents' relationship to their own children.

Third, you have to look at the possibility that if your life has arrived at a point where you frequently experience feelings of boredom, uselessness and loneliness, then you may feel that your grandparenthood has presented you with an opportunity to be busy and useful and involved. On another level, the lonely little child in yourself, feeling forlorn and left out, may see a new and ready-made family to be a part of again. If your needs are strong enough, you can rationalize that your son or daughter needs your help and thus make yourself insensitive to your child's signals that you are more involved than he wants you to be. One grandmother I know didn't get the message until her child and grandchild were almost always out when they knew she was probably coming to call.

Finally, because of the sweet and close interaction with your grandchild, you may often be tempted to enter into a near conspiracy against his parents. ("I'll buy you an ice cream cone, and we won't say a word about it to your mommy or daddy, okay?") Since your inner child would be greatly involved in this, your relationship with your grandchildren would have aspects of two children playing and being rebellious. This is an abdication of your adult wisdom and cannot be good for your grandchild or your relations with your own child. It is the type of interaction that leads to our recognition of the truth in that old joke, "Why do grandparents and their grandchildren get along so well?" Answer: "Because they both have a common enemy."

Of course there are instances when it may be the young parents who make themselves into the enemy. The understandable desire they may have to insulate somewhat the new family from the world and to separate themselves from their past role as someone's children so that they can more fully assume their role as someone's parents may go too far. They may greatly restrict the grandparents' visits, may try to instruct the grandparents on every detail of how they are to act with their grandchild and may be hostile toward their parents at the slightest sign that their parents want to have more to do with the grandchild or if the grandparents make any moves that have not been previously okayed. It is as if the inner child of the young parents is saying, "Now I'm grown up, I'm a parent myself, and I'm in charge. So you better do it my way or else."

If your child is acting this way with you, you know he has discovered that he has an enormously powerful weapon in his own unresolved conflicts with you, and that weapon is your grandchild. Your child knows how special that grandchild is to you and he can, in essence, threaten that if you don't behave yourself, your relationship with him will be even more limited. And a grandchild of almost any age can sense when he is caught and being used in family hostilities.

What can you do if you have looked at the situation and yourself as honestly as you can, perhaps with the help of an objective observer, and have concluded that you have not been too intrusive, have not usurped parental prerogatives, have acknowledged your child's authority with your grandchild, and yet still find your relationship with your grandchild is being interfered with by your son or daughter? As always, it is important to keep your inner child out of it, to be able to take a position that says, "Listen, I have no wish to invade your parental territory—and I acknowledge it is your territory completely—but I want you to know that my feelings about Bobby (or Barbie) are very special and I take great pleasure from being with him. Please don't use him in any old conflicts you have with me. It's not fair to me or to him. Let's try to work this out so he and I can have a relationship you can feel comfortable with." Or words to that effect.

Now, let's be clear on something. If you don't have a burning desire to be a grandparent or if you aren't absolutely wild about your grandchild and don't want to spend half your time being with him and the other half bragging out him, it doesn't mean something is terribly wrong with you. It could mean that your life is so rich and busy that while your children and grandchildren are a pleasant part of it, they are not the major part. And that's okay. Or it could mean that you have simply had enough of the role of child-rearer and nurturer and you just couldn't burp or powder another baby, nor can you still honestly wax ecstatic about your grandchild's first step, word, tooth, day at school, date or whatever. There is a scene in Tillie Olsen's remarkable short story, *Tell Me a Riddle,* in which Ma, who has raised a houseful of kids and now has grandchildren all over the country and has always been an earth mother to all of them, has been coerced by her husband to take a trip to the coast to see their newest grandchild. The baby is put in her arms with the expectation by all that it would be an instant replay of an old, tender scene. "A new baby. How many warm, seductive babies. She holds him stiffly *away* from her, so that he wails. And a long shudder begins, and the sweat beads on her forehead."* Ma has had it. She wants to be home, nurturing her own tired self.

No, you don't have to be a stereotyped "granny" or "gramps" or whatever terms are used in your ethnic heritage. Certainly there is nothing wrong if you don't want to baby-sit with your grandchild. You can well feel that you've done your stint and you are now in a new stage of life. Perhaps you finally have the leisure to travel, to study or to pursue recreations and hobbies. You are entitled to that.

Can such "ungrandparental" feelings indicate you have some

* Tillie Olsen, *Tell Me a Riddle* (New York: Delacorte, 1960).

problem in your own development? Yes, at times. For example, if you are so concerned not to be seen as older and to remain eternally young that you don't yet want grandchildren even though they are here or on their way, then you are not facing the reality of your age. If you have grandchildren, then you are old enough to have grandchildren. It is your inner child who wants to be forever the ingenue or forever Peter Pan, and this can keep you from gracefully accepting who you really are at that moment. Grandparents don't have to be old, doddering rocking-chair jockeys. You can be youthful and active and still own up to the role of grandparent.

There can be a similar problem in your own development if you have trouble entering into any real relationship with your grandchild. You will have to search yourself to see if it indicates whether the self-centered child inside you has taken over, limiting your capacity to be a loving person. Is it simply that you are at a point in your life where you no longer wish to be involved with the care of small children, or have you become so focused on your own pains or pleasures that you can't care about anything or anyone outside that sphere? Only you can see the dividing line and decide what you want to do about it.

Grandparenthood, too, has its stages. As the grandchildren grow up, your relationship with them is less and less determined by their parents. They can make their own arrangements to be with you or to choose not to be with you. And you can have the joy of opening new experiences for them. In *Evergreen,* Anna has taken her granddaughter Laura to a matinee ballet. They had a "lovely, lovely day" and now are returning home. Laura says to her, "You know, Nana, I'll remember today. I'll say to my grandchildren, the first time I saw *Swan Lake* I went with my grandmother. It was a beautiful warm afternoon and we rode together on the train."*

It is not always so idyllic. For one thing, as your grandchild gets older, he may no longer see you in that idealized, glowing way he did when he was a child. His view of you will be more and more based on how he perceives you as a person and not a role. This means you may be judged—and found wanting. And

* Belva Plain, *Evergreen,* p. 526.

this in turn means you must take full responsibility for who you are with him. You can't have his goodwill forever based on past ice cream cones or trips to the zoo. You may do things that turn your grandchild off, as when one grandmother sent her granddaughter a set of beautiful, personalized stationery for her thirteenth birthday, and the granddaughter was delighted till she saw that all the envelopes were already addressed, with grandma's address! This grandmother had no one to blame but herself for her grandchild's now withdrawing to a greater distance from her. The possessive inner child in the grandmother had emerged, and her granddaughter didn't like it.

But even if you do nothing to push your grandchildren away, the natural developments of their lives will make them less available to you. When they become adolescents, they are less likely to be as ambivalent and rebellious with you as with their parents, but the sheer busyness of their day-to-day activities will create some distance. One woman in her late seventies told me, "Of course there was pleasure from my grandchildren, baby-sitting for them and all. Then they really clung to you. But once they get older it's not the same. Only when they're small. Then they're adorable, they're close to you. They get older, they're grown-up, they're adults—they send me a card. One would never call; now he'll call me once in a blue moon or send me a check. But otherwise they don't bother with me. And they are adorable . . . they're so sweet, but I never see them."

It happens like that, often. If you react to it with your possessive inner child, you will suffer unnecessary feelings of rejection and hurt and may react in bitter ways that damage your relationship with your grandchild. But if you see this separation as part of the normal and healthy development of your grandchild, you can take pleasure in his expanding self, and at the same time you can let yourself realize that none of those beautiful times of special closeness has been lost on your grandchild. They live in his memories and even deeper than his memories. Those incomparable moments have become part of who he is—which means that you are forever part of who he is. Your appreciation of that can be and should be a source of warm satisfaction for you, now and as the years go by.

CHAPTER 9

As Time Goes By

Some "passages" parents encounter are occasioned, as we have seen, by steps our children take, such as when they marry or present us with grandchildren. But there are other parental passages that are products of stages in your own life. These include being single again (through divorce or being widowed), remarriage, retirement and aging. These are common phases of the life cycle, and each will influence and be influenced by our relationship with our grown-up children.

Alone Again, Naturally

A recently widowed woman of fifty-eight told me, "When Al died, I was alone for the first time in my life. I went from my parents to Al. We started going with each other in my junior year in high school. The phrase then was that we were 'keeping company.' We got married two years after I graduated, and we had the three girls. A few years ago, when the last one left home to get married, we both began to go through that 'empty nest syndrome,' but then we came to really enjoy just being with each other, without the responsibilities of the kids. We decided to keep the house even though it was so big. . . . Then Al died so suddenly. One day he was here and the next day he was gone and I was alone. The kids were 100 percent with me that first week or two, but then it was me and the emptiest house in the world. . . . My daughters keep in touch. Two of them live pretty far away and we talk on the phone at least once a week. The one who lives the closest—my middle daughter—we get together, but she has her own family. I never thought of killing myself, but at times the loneliness is so awful I thought I would die from it."

Her words will strike a resonant chord in many of you whose marriages have ended one way or another and whose children are now grown. We've talked often in the book of the inner child's fear of abandonment, and here the worst has happened; your mate is gone and your children have lives quite apart from you. That little child within you will come to the surface, raw with all the feelings of desolation, of sadness at the loss of those loving attachments and of fear that the aloneness will go on forever. You may reach for your grown-up children then, wanting their closeness and nurturance. And usually your grown-up children will respond, being there for you during the immediate grief and mourning, then, at some time and in varying degrees, returning to the pre-tragedy course of their lives.

For how long can a parent who has become suddenly alone expect his children to play a consistent nurturing role? Mrs. March, a woman in her sixties, told me that her daughter, a woman of forty-three with two children, said to her just three days after Mrs. March's husband died, "Mother, you'll have to stand on your own two feet. I have my own family to attend to." And she went her way, keeping a "polite" contact. Certainly three days of attentiveness is very brief, far less than a person usually needs in mourning the loss of a spouse, and doubtless there is a history between this mother and daughter which might help explain what appears as an unfeeling abandonment. But it is a short, short time. Mrs. March later said, "In your book, write about being widowed. A parent really needs his children close then. It doesn't mean they'll have to take care of you forever, but they must help their mother in the first year." A year? What kind of help? And what does it mean that Mrs. March says "they must"?

When a parent is suddenly alone and the child inside the parent wants most to reach out to his offspring, these offspring, perhaps having struggled to achieve the independence they now have, perhaps still struggling to keep some sense of order and harmony in their own lives, can become terrified that their parent's grief and aloneness will impel this parent to depend heavily on them. The inner child of the offspring, who always harbors some of the early fears of being engulfed or controlled by his parent, is threatened by his parent's new neediness. He is afraid of too much closeness, too much fusion, and of the loss of his hard-won boundaries. These sons and daughters may then react in ways that seem callous, even cruel. And at times they are indeed callous and cruel.

There are no rules as to how devoted a grown-up child should be to a parent now alone. Sometimes, in retrospect, the parent may realize that in his fear and grief, he was asking too much. One woman said, "My husband died just about a year or two after my son had moved out into a place of his own in the city. I said, 'Lenny, come back to live with me. You can have your own life and I'll have someone in the house.' But he said, 'No, I'm not sitting on the couch with you, watching TV when everyone's downtown.' I wasn't happy about it, but he was right and I was wrong. I got out and made a life for myself. I became active in the church and I made friends." Later I asked her what she would want to say to a parent who becomes widowed, and she said, "The main thing is to let go of the kids. Don't go out with them Saturdays or Sundays. Today, all my friends are people I met in the six years since my husband died."

Each situation is different. Each parent's relationship with each child is different. If you have been very close to a grown-up child and you each have been able to be there for the other, the chances are you can count on his being dependable and helpful to you in a fairly sustained way as compared to a child whose relationship has been distant or antagonistic. But certain guidelines can be helpful.

1. When you have suffered the loss of a spouse, it is all right and natural to allow the hurt, scared, needy child inside you to

emerge for a while and to want to lean on certain people. These other people can be "auxiliary life support systems," like the extra tank of oxygen a diver may turn to if the first tank is cut off.

2. It is understandable that one of your auxiliary life support systems will be your children, and it is okay to ask them to be there for you for a while. (Whether they will and how they will depends on the nature of your relationship, the type of person your child is, and what your child's life circumstances are at that time.)

3. It is important to recognize that the inner child of your son or daughter has also come forward, not just in reaction to his own loss, but with one of the main childhood fears of being swallowed up and losing independence. In recognizing this, you might be able to say to your child, "I'll need you close for a little while, and I'll need help with a few things, but you needn't be afraid of it because I want to get on my own two feet as soon as I can."

4. During the period when you need those auxiliary life support systems, spread that need over a few people—not just your children or one particular child. It is a time when you should feel free to call on a little help from your friends.

5. If your period of dependency is prolonged, stretching into months, then it is most likely to be resented by your son or daughter as intrusive, and even more important, it is bad for your own development. It means that you have given over so much control to your needy inner child that you are becoming too passive and dependent to start a new vibrant and effective chapter in your life. When your feeling of being lost and leaning on others seems to hang on, seek out a self-help widows' group or have a professional consultation.

There are somewhat different problems presented when your singlehood is brought about by your divorcing rather than being widowed. Some parents, when they have gotten divorced after their children are adults, are still afraid of the upsetting effect it will have on their children; others believe it will not be upsetting to their children and are surprised to find that it is. The truth is, it often does disturb the grown-up children to some degree, but they are usually quite understanding of the circumstances and though saddened, think it's a good idea. Elsewhere I have quoted the reactions of a young woman who was away at college when she got the news that her parents, married almost thirty-five years, had separated.

> I felt terrible, like the rug had been pulled out from under me. But then I noticed I also felt relieved. At first I couldn't understand that, but as I thought about it I realized it was no accident that my parents split up so soon after I went to college. My older brother and sister had been out long before so I was the last one at home, and it was clear that the children were the reason they had hung together. Somewhere inside me I must have always known that, and the relief I felt was of no longer being burdened by that awesome responsibility of keeping two people together who didn't belong together. I also realized how much of my personality had developed around that task. So I felt lost, confused, very sad, and liberated.*

Though it can be upsetting to adult children when their parents divorce, it does not really affect their lives very much and should never be a reason for parents not to divorce when everything else points to its being a good idea. If they use that rationalization, they may become like the subjects of the grim joke about the couple in their mid-nineties who consult a lawyer about a divorce. Why, he wants to know, after more than seventy years should they suddenly come to this decision. "It wasn't sudden," the aged husband answers. "We've hated each other almost from the beginning, but we made up our minds not to get a divorce till the children were dead!"

Depending on the circumstances of the divorce, you may feel good or just awful. A divorce is always the death of a dream that started off with hope, and when the marriage has been long, it can be followed by a period of bereavement as deep as at a death and a period of bitterness that can be deeper and longer lasting than at a death. Again, if you are in this position, we can expect that your inner child will be howling in grief and anger, and that you will tend to turn to your children for support. As with being widowed, this is an appropriate transient stage. But if you require

* Howard Halpern, *Cutting Loose,* p. 186.

that your children support you *against* their other parent—that they must agree that what he did was horrendous, that he is an awful person, that he is completely at fault, or that they now limit their relationship with that parent—then the child within you has taken over too much, and you have abdicated your role as a caring parent. A mature and caring parent does not require his offspring to oppose, criticize or limit contact with his child's other parent just because of the way that person has behaved about the marriage. The child of any age should be free to retain a relationship with both his mother and father if he should want it, without being made to feel he is disloyal to the other.

Here I Go Again

The single parent of grown-up children may choose not to remain single. What impact does his remarriage have on his adult children? Sometimes, very little. But it is surprising how often these children do react strongly. They may see their parent's new spouse as a replacement of the other parent and pass judgment accordingly. The adult daughters in the movie *Interiors* knew their mother was very disturbed but saw her as an elegant, well-read woman of fine taste, and when their father divorced their mother and later married a hearty, more flashy and less refined woman, they reacted to her with disgust and anger. It is as if the little child within them, and particularly within one daughter, were saying, "She isn't good enough to take my Mommy's place. She isn't good enough for my wonderful Daddy. If he marries her he is leaving me!"

Parents can listen to their children's reaction, but in the long run, only the parent can know what he needs in a mate at this time in his life. So give yourself some time to digest and appraise your children's negative judgment to see if, in their knowledge of you and their view of your contemplated partner, they see something you do not (after all, love can be blind at any age) or if they are reacting with their critical inner child. If you decide that you would be happy taking this step, it would be folly to let your children's evaluation stop you, particularly since their admonition may be coming from their inner child who may want you to be dependently close to them or to remain forever loyal to the departed parent.

You can't demand that your grown-up children like your new spouse, let alone love him. Permit them to have their own feelings and develop their own relationship with this person. But you can demand that your spouse be treated courteously because you would not want to subject your new marriage partner or yourself to uncivil or pointedly cold reactions. This does not mean automatically taking your mate's side in every conflict—you do want to preserve a good relationship with your children—but you may have to distance your children if the inner child in them has taken over so much that they give you both a chronic hard time.

Though there can be these negative reactions, most of the time the new spouse will be welcomed by the children, first as someone their parent cares about and later as someone they may come to love very deeply. I have seen it happen often, where this step-parent of the children's later years expands the children's feelings of being parented and makes them aware of the specific things they can get in the new relationship. Partly because this relationship is free of an early history of conflicts, it can sometimes be quite close and caring. If the other original parent is still around, we can only hope that his or her inner child would not lead him to act jealously or competitively with this step-parent.

Up the Lazy River

One common parental passage in the later years is *retirement.* Usually this means that the family breadwinner or breadwinners terminate the work that had been the source of a livelihood for many years. Why may this retirement of the parents be an issue in their relationship with their adult children? There are several reasons.

First, there are times when the parents may move far away, such as to a sunny clime, thus changing the nature and frequency of their contact with their children. Whereas before they may have spoken on the phone several times a week and seen each other every few weeks, there may now be letters, occasional phone calls and annual visits. Depending on the relationship, the parents, the child or both can experience this anywhere from a deprivation to a blessing. Problems sometimes come up around the parents' wanting the children to spend every vacation with them and the children's wanting to vary their vacations and do something different. It is then very tempting for parents to try to get their way by provoking guilt ("We're not getting any younger, you know") and for children to get into either a compliant Song and Dance about it—by visiting but being sullen, barely civil, and leaving early—or a defiant Song and Dance by almost totally avoiding visiting. The relationship would go much better if the parents, putting aside their own clinging inner child were simply to say, "We'd love to have you visit on such and such a time. If you can't make it or have other plans, we will try again another time. Or if you want to drop by for a day or two on the way to somewhere else, it would be good to see you." Where there has been a Song and Dance going on around this issue, ending it in this way is likely to make the visits more frequent and certainly more pleasant.

Particularly when parents have retired to the sun belt, they often have their grandchildren visit them on school vacations. This can be delightful for both. Problems can arise when the retired parents feel their children are sending the grandchildren as substitutes for themselves or when the grandchildren get older and prefer to do other things. Again, it is important for the parents to see the invitation they proffer as just that, an invitation, not a demand. The children or grandchildren have the right to say no. The sum total of all their feelings in the relationship and of the nature of their lives at that moment will determine the response. Sometimes the opposite problem arises when the retired parents feel the grandchildren are "dumped" on them or that the children visit only to use the facilities for a cheap vacation. It is important for the retired parents to realize it is their lives and their home and that they have a right to say no and set some ground rules for the visits.

A second area of possible problems arising out of parental retirement can occur when the retired parents need financial help from their children. The children may feel burdened by it, the parents may feel bad about needing it, and it can become an uncomfortable situation. As with all money issues, it is best if it is planned for in advance, the terms of the arrangement set down very explicitly, the acceptance of the arrangement truly mutual, and no hidden strings attached that can lead to a Money Minuet (see Chapter 3).

The third and most common arena of conflict spawned by retirement comes from the parents suddenly not having anything to do. They are at loose ends, and like little children at home on a rainy day who turn to their parents and say, "What should I play? What should I draw? Play with me," these retired parents may find themselves now going to their children in just this way. They may want their children to fill in the slack of their now long and unscheduled days, and their children may not wish to do this nor be free to do this. It can become a tense and frustrating situation for all.

That is why it is crucial for parents, preferably long before they retire, to plan a life that will not leave them so restless and shiftless that they turn to their children for too much of their companionship and pastime needs. The necessity to plan and create the retirement years is spelled out constructively in Peter Schwed's book, *Hanging In There,** subtitled, *How to Resist Retirement from Life and Avoid Being Put Out to Pasture*. What I find remarkable about this book is not only the helpful things the author says about the retirement years, but what he does *not* say. He managed to write a book chock full of both inspiration and practical details and *never once* wrote a word about the retiree's children! Since I know that the author has four adult children and an enviable relationship with them, I was a bit surprised, and even more surprised that it had never occurred to him. What he is telling us through this omission is that the planning and enjoyment of the retirement years should not be focused on one's children, or on one's role as parent. Instead he asks, "Is it possible that now for the very first time in your entire life when you are neither pressed by obligations, nor appear to be needed very much any longer, you can see opportunities, set goals, achieve attainments that consciously or unconsciously you have always wanted to try, and never could? My answer to that is a ringing YES. . . . "†

* Peter Schwed, *Hanging In There* (Boston: Houghton-Mifflin, 1977).

† *Ibid.*, p. 4.

It is easy to see that this approach, besides being a positive, active and vital approach to this phase of life, would enable you to avoid all kinds of draining and unsatisfying Songs and Dances with your children. In fact, it will probably benefit your relationship with them enormously, because instead of approaching them like a shiftless child saying, "I'm bored. You must play with me," you would meet them from your own feeling of excitement and involvement, which will make you an interesting person with whom to be.

Red Sails in the Sunset

When do you consider yourself "old"? Is it when you pass a landmark date? Sixty? The traditional sixty-five? Seventy? When you get senior citizen privileges or your hair is all snow or your body increasingly betrays you? Or is it when you look in the mirror and see a face that, on anyone else, you would instantly think of as old? For some it comes on suddenly—perhaps an illness or disability drives the point home. For others it is a slow awareness, a gradual development.

As you have been aging, your children have also. If you consider yourself old, the chances are that you have children who are middle-aged. How is it going between you and the middle-aged people you still call your "children"?

All too often, your needs as an aging person will clash with the place where your children are in their lives. You may feel more needy and dependent than in many years. Perhaps you are alone, perhaps not working, many of your friends and siblings may be gone, and you may feel the effects of infirmities, some of them incapacitating. These factors and the dependence on others they can bring stimulate all those inner child feelings of helplessness, not being in good control of your body functions, inadequacy and dependency. There can be a reversal of roles, as you wish to lean on your children the way they once leaned on you. Or as Edith Stern has written, "The facts of life are more than the process of reproduction. It is equally a fact of life that in the course of time the roles of parents and children become reversed, and the younger must take care of the elder."*

* Edith M. Stern with Mabel Ross, *You and Your Aging Parents* (New York: Harper & Row, 1965), p. 9.

It doesn't always happen this way. People often remain vigorous, active and independent well into years that may be considered ancient for, as we will see, how one ages can be very much a product of a person's total approach to life. But frequently enough, this reversal occurs at a time in the life of your children when these needs of yours are difficult to encompass, if not downright unwelcome. They may be just at the tail end of launching their own children, perhaps still dealing with adolescent storms, or struggling to meet college expenses, or more likely, for the first time in decades they feel free of such responsibilities and able to relax and selfishly think only of themselves. And suddenly new responsibilities and new limitations are occasioned by the needs that may arise from your aging. The stage is set for an old but ever sad conflict. Here is how one woman in her eighties, living alone in a city apartment, experiences it.

> All in all, should I be sick tomorrow, which has happened . . . no one came near me. None of my children came. I fell down last week, I fell in the gutter. I hurt both my knees. Some woman met my son and she said to him, "You know your mother fell down and hurt her knees." No one came to see how I was hurt or was I hurt that bad, was I hurt so that I couldn't move. No, there is absolutely no feeling, no regard. I can't understand why. When five children live together under one roof, sleep in one bed . . . All right, they all went their own way, true; this one did this and this one did this, and we expect that. They got married, they have families, fine. I have twelve grandchildren—they should live and be well—but even my grandchildren! What does it mean? What does it mean for a son, no matter how busy he is—I know he is busy, but he's got a desk and he's got a phone—to call only once a week? I am disillusioned, I am. I didn't expect to end my life like this. But you know, my husband—he was a foreigner—his ideas were, of course, different from mine. But we used to sit and discuss the future like husbands and wives do sometimes. I'd say, "Oh, I have five children so I'm all right." You see, I was an only child. That's why I wanted a big family. He'd say to me, "Dear, you have five children so you've got five doors to get thrown out of." He used that as a joke. But it's very hard.

She has made her feelings very clear. "I am disillusioned. I am." The underlying theme I hear from many aged people is that they were so much there for their children when their children needed them, but there is little reciprocity now. And it is not only the little inner child in these parents who is crying out, but in many instances it is also the mature parent who is unhappy at a real absence of closeness and concern on the part of these children. They may be confused and bitter because they may have been much more involved with their own aged parents than their children are now with them. This same woman said:

> My mother was a widow. She lived with us for twenty years. She didn't read or write. I don't have to tell you, but I was everything to her. She died in my arms. I wouldn't put her in the hospital; I took her home. She died in my bedroom, in my arms. That's why I feel, Why? And my children saw it; they were growing up with her. So they'd seen everything. . . . So I can't be such a terrible person. They've never said I was a terrible person or that they were angry at me. And it's not the money end of it. They're just too busy. If only each one would come up once a week and sit with me and have a cup of coffee with me and discuss the rest of the family. . . . You know what it is? It's a lack of love.

Again, her words sting. "It's a lack of love." How is this woman, whose mother died in her arms after living with her for twenty years, to understand children who rarely call, who do not visit even after hearing she was hurt? Much of the answer probably lies in the whole history of her relationship with them and the feelings that developed within this family. Perhaps it was never particularly warm or loving. Perhaps there was much rivalry, antagonism or anger. Or perhaps the children were spoiled and not instilled with a mature sense of responsibility and concern. But part of the answer—perhaps the major part—is that this society has changed dramatically in its view of family and obligations to parents since this woman was young. In her youth, the younger was generally expected to take care of the older in a very close, direct way. There were fewer alternatives; retirement communities, old age communities and nursing homes were rare. Medical science had not become so complex that many older people needed to be in a professional treatment setting as is true now. There was less mobility in her time; families stayed closer together. And there was less emphasis then on pursuing your own personal fulfillment—"doing your own thing." So this woman's expectations of how it would be when she told her husband, "Oh, I have five children so I'm all right" met some cold realities of another set of values and circumstances. This societal change is behind a lot of the pain and despair many elderly feel.

Are these middle-aged children who have disappointed their elderly parents' expectations "bad"? Not really. Some of them may be terribly self-centered people, but many are quite kind and unselfish in other areas of their life, such as with their own spouses or children, or in community activities. Again, each parent-child history is unique, but it will be helpful for you as an aged parent, or one who expects to be someday, to understand their feelings about having a parent who is well on in years. As we have seen, your needs as an elderly person may come at a time in their lives when they are totally involved in other developments. They may have struggled long and hard to be free of certain demands both from outside themselves and from an inner child who always made them be more appeasing and self-denying than they wanted to be.

And there can be other feelings about your advancing years that may be going on in your child. He may not want to face the fact of your aging. In one of the most helpful and sensitive books on aging, the authors write:

> Most of us, as children, viewed our parents as immortal—strong enough to protect us forever. As we mature we learn we can take care of ourselves and in the process find out, with some regret, that our parents are not quite as perfect or infallible as we once thought. Somewhere inside us, however, remains a trace of the old conviction that our parents could still protect us if we needed them to. . . . On an intellectual level we keep telling ourselves, "It's understandable—they're getting old, they're fading." But on the gut level we can still be sad, frightened, resentful as if they had broken a promise to us. . . . Every time we see them we have to be reminded of their mortality—and our own.*

* Barbara Silverstone and Helen Kandel Hyman, *You and Your Aging Parent* (New York: Pantheon, 1976), p. 25.

Your child may be so threatened by your aging, because his inner child wants you to be the eternally strong and capable parent, that he may deny both your aging and your changing needs because of the aging. Again, let us turn to the wisdom of Erma Bombeck. In a piece called "When Did I Become the Mother and the Mother Become the Child" she talks of the gradual reversal of roles, of how she finds herself saying things to her mother that she can remember her mother's saying to her when she was a little girl, such as, "How can I give you a home permanent if you won't sit still? If you don't care how you look, I do!" or "So where's the sweater? You know how cold the stores get with air conditioning. That's the last thing you need is a cold," or "Do you have to go to the bathroom before we go?" When did the change happen? ". . . did it come the rainy afternoon when you were driving home from the store and you slammed on your brakes and your arms sprang protectively between her and the windshield and your eyes met with a knowing, sad look?" Then Erma Bombeck ends with a few short paragraphs that capture the sadness the middle-aged daughter feels at the change and her keen awareness of her own aging.

> You bathe and pat dry the body that once housed you. You spoon-feed the lips that kissed your cuts and bruises and made them well. You comb the hair that used to playfully cascade over you to make you laugh. You arrange the covers over legs that once carried you high into the air to Banbury Cross.
>
> The naps are frequent as yours used to be. You accompany her to the bathroom and wait to return her to bed. She has a sitter already for New Year's Eve. You never thought it would be like this.
>
> While riding with your daughter one day, she slams on her brakes and her arm flies out instinctively in front of you between the windshield and your body.
>
> My God. So Soon.*

Your aging, then, can be painful to your children and they may react with a combination of compassion and avoidance. This is

* Erma Bombeck, *If Life Is a Bowl of Cherries,* p. 184.

particularly true around the subject of death. One woman of seventy-nine told me, in speaking of her son, "You can't talk to him about death or anything. This is the worst thing you can talk about. They don't want to hear about it, and I want to talk about it. I want to tell them what to do. So I tell them if anything happens, the deed to the plot is in the vault, so you'll know where to go. But they don't want to talk about it. If you ignore it, it goes away. I have to keep saying everything is fine."

Not being able to talk about some of the facts and concerns of your aging and of the approach of death with your children can increase your sense of isolation and loneliness. You may well find this type of avoidance frustrating and silly, and in a way it is, but it can be helpful if you see it arising out of the little girl or boy in your grown-up child who does not want to face your mortality or his own and who may feel unable to deal with the feelings it triggers.

Will You Still Need Me, Will You Still Feed Me, When I'm Sixty-Four

Despite all these complex emotional matters, there are many adult children who are really committed to their aged parents in a reliable and loving way. When I've talked to some middle-aged people whose lives clearly include caring for elderly parents, certain consistent themes come up.

> I really love my dad because of the kind of man he is and the kind of father he's been. Devoting this much time to him now when he can't take care of himself the way he used to feels right and natural. It's what I want to do. In fact, I couldn't do it any other way.

> It's no pleasure, believe me, but I feel a sense of obligation. I believe this is the way people should be. It's like a duty.

> It's turned my whole life inside out, and my family's, but I have to, or I would feel so guilty I couldn't live with myself.

Devoted love, obligation and guilt are the themes that emerge to explain why much of the current lives of those adult offspring are centered around their old parents. It certainly seemed to me that the parents whose children were with them out of a simple loving response would experience what they are receiving differently from those whose children responded out of duty or guilt. In actuality, most children's motives were a mixture of the three feelings, and their actions were tempered by the realities of their lives and by the presence and nature of previous Songs and Dances. It is a difficult situation for the children as well as the parents, and I wrote the following guidelines for these *grown-up children*.

1. Although your parents' part of an old Song and Dance is likely to be exacerbated by the aging process, they now may have new needs which do not necessarily reflect the old manipulations.

2. It will be important for you to discern how much of their behavior is an attempt to revive or continue an old Song and Dance and how much is a legitimate function of their diminished capacities.

3. You are likely to respond helpfully more willingly if your parent is not expressing his needs in terms of an old Song and Dance. For example, complaints of neglect from a parent who has played martyr ever since you can remember will probably make you feel more antagonistic than the same complaints from a parent who was never a complainer.

4. It would be better for everyone if you can allow your parents' *real needs* to bring out your compassion, not treating those needs as inappropriate demands, and not by responding from your own frightened or angry or self-indulgent inner child.

5. You will have to use your mature caring and your adult judgment (and not the guilt or submission or your inner child) to decide not what you *should* do but what is *best* to do. You must take into account your parents' needs, health and personality as well as your own, the needs of your family, and the realities of your resources.

6. While aging and illness may bring your parent's inner child to the surface, that child is not all of him. It will be important to encourage as much independence on his part as is possible.*

I would give similar counsel to the aging parent. I would advise you to be aware of the Songs and Dances you have played with your children and to make every effort not to repeat them now, lest you find yourself in the hapless position of the boy who cried wolf too often. If you've always been a complainer, or a fear-inspiring big boss, or a guilt-provoking martyr, or a shame-stimulating moralizer, or any other role that came from your inner child, then *now,* when the importance of effectively communicating your needs is greater than ever, using the same tactics may not work. It will be up to you to find a new way, a way to directly and effectively state your needs without the old demands or manipulations. If for decades you have been saying things like, "I was in such agony but you didn't care enough to call," then how is your child to know that you aren't inviting him to the same old Song and Dance if you say it again? But if you can see how destructive and self-defeating the Song and Dance has been, you then might be able to say, as one man I know did, "Listen, I know I've been a big complainer and made you feel guilty a lot. I don't want to do that. The fact is, I have real troubles now and I can't do as much for myself as I used to, so if you could take me to the doctor every Tuesday afternoon, I would appreciate it very much." It is never too late to stop an old Song and Dance and to begin a more honest interaction.

Besides recognizing that the old Songs and Dances may be getting in the way, it is important to let yourself see and acknowledge the great changes in what our society expects of a child's obligation to his aged parent. You may not like these changes, but they have happened, and your child's not being available to you in the same way as you were available to your parent does not necessarily mean that your child is selfish or unfeeling, or

* Derived from a chapter about the expectant heir (Parent-Child Relationships That Affect the Will) in Martin Levin's book, *What's Happening to Your Inheritance* (New York: Times Books, 1979).

there is a "lack of love." Recognizing this can alleviate many painful feelings that you are unloved or that you raised an awful person. It is a matter of changing your expectations to fit current realities. One woman of seventy-eight said, "They have their own lives to live. I have to adjust not to expect too much, and then I won't be disappointed." She indicated that this lowering of expectations was very difficult, but the more she succeeded in it and focused instead on involving herself with other activities, the less she suffered about her children's not being with her as much as she had hoped.

But it is not just a matter of current realities. Wise people have known for centuries that there are limits to the appropriate demands the older generation may make on the younger. Glückel Von Hameln lived in Germany from 1644 to 1724. In Yiddish, she wrote the following portion of her memoirs in 1690:

> . . . We should, I say, put ourselves to great pains for our children, for on this the world is built, yet we must understand that if children did as much for their parents, the children would quickly tire of it.
>
> A bird once set out to cross a windy sea with its three fledglings. The sea was so wide and the wind so strong, the father bird was forced to carry his young, one by one, in his strong claws. When he was halfway across with the first fledgling the wind turned to a gale, and he said, "My child, look how I am struggling and risking my life in your behalf. When you are grown up, will you do as much for me and provide for my old age?" The fledgling replied, "Only bring me to safety, and when you are old I shall do everything you ask of me." Whereas the father bird dropped his child into the sea, and it drowned, and he said, "So it shall be done to such a liar as you." Then the father bird returned to shore, set forth with his second fledgling, asked the same question, and receiving the same answer, drowned the second child with the cry, "You, too, are a liar!" Finally he set out with the third fledgling, and when he asked the same question, the third and last fledgling replied, "My dear father, it is true you are struggling mightily and risking your life in my behalf, and I shall be wrong not to repay you when you are old, but I cannot bind myself. This though I

> can promise: when I am grown up and have children of my own, I shall do as much for them as you have done for me." Whereupon the father bird said, "Well spoken, my child, and wisely; your life I will spare and I will carry you to shore in safety."*

Thus she points to the parents' obligation to care for and raise up the child. This is not only a moral imperative, but a biological imperative if the human race is to survive. But for the young to take care of the old is not the same obligation. "I shall be wrong not to repay you when you are old, but I cannot bind myself." Caring for one's parents becomes, then, an ethical matter, a human relations issue, but does not have the binding power of an imperative related to the sustaining of the race, an imperative that must always look forward and not back.

So where does this leave the aging parent? If his child has no obligation to care for him that arises out of biology, if his child was brought up in a world with limited expectations about his responsibilities to his parents, if his child has been put off by past Songs and Dances so that he is now distant and hostile, then what does an aging parent do about his needs for care and closeness?

We have already seen the importance of shifting your expectations and discontinuing Songs and Dances that interfere with direct and loving communication. Those are essential steps. But there are other steps that can be just as important.

• You must not put all your needs in your child's basket. It may be too much of a burden for your child and make you as dependent on this one person as a junkie is on his fix. It is never too late to make new friends or to revive relationships with old friends and relatives.

• Don't build your relationships primarily around your suffering. I have seen parents offer their pain to their children as if it were a precious gift. Your pain is real, and must oft be acknowledged, but it's no gift. You have much more to offer than that.

* Glückel Von Hameln, *The Memoirs* (New York: Behrman House, Inc.), p. 2.

• Avoid as much as possible being in the position of the passive child. Sometimes your children will try to put you in that position, making too much of a role reversal of it out of their need to be in control. You may be old and need some care, but you're not a baby. Don't make yourself one or let them make you one.

• Do not let your child be condescending to you. One woman told me that her son said, "If you're a good girl, I'll visit you next week." She was able to say, "If you think of me as a little girl who has to be good in order for you to visit, then I'd rather not have you come." Those were brave words, considering her loneliness, but her self-respect came first. And he did visit—respectfully.

• Live as fully and as independently as you possibly can. Disheartened by some of the losses in your capacities and the changes in your life, you can tend to vegetate. Besides the fact that such resignation from life is self-destructive, perhaps even suicidal, it places a heavy burden on your relationship with your child. Nobody, not even the most loving child, wants to be with someone who says "No" to every suggestion that you move toward interests and vitality and life. You may have much more capacity for a stimulating and independent life than you are living. Instead of leaning on your children to give meaning to your life, now is the time to call upon your old skills or to develop new skills, to continue old hobbies or learn new ones, to do volunteer work or remunerative work if you are at all able, to involve yourself in group activity, worthy causes, and learning. As the saying goes, "Keep learning as if you'll live forever, and keep living as if you'll die tomorrow."

• Recognize that although your child's first duty is to himself and his children, and that you may have expectations of him that are out of keeping with his view of what is called for, this does not mean you have no claim on him. It does not mean you must crawl into the molding or be a smiling and accepting Kewpie doll or an undemanding shadow of a person, grateful for minimal attentions. You have a history with your child. You are something to each other. You have given much. You have a right to ask something out of the history and nature of your relationship. And if there are problems in that relationship that stand in the way of an easy flow of caring, you may regret that you did not improve the relationship before it had to sustain the additional burdens of your aging. But you will never be too old to make the relationship more real, more open and more loving.

CHAPTER 10

Of Thee I Sing

I was startled when I first read of Barry Stevens's referring to her "ex-son." She explained her use of the term this way: "John is forty years old. On paper, he is my son. On paper, that goes on forever. I don't have to live with that paper identification. When I don't think of him as my son, I am free of all the personal junk in my head connected with 'my son.' . . . When I don't think of myself as mother or of him as son, I like what happens. There is no demand—no need for more."*

Her words were exciting and disturbing. I liked her attempt to go beyond labels, to deal with the essence of what the relationship is that exists right now between two adults, Barry and John, rather than mother and son. But I didn't like the implication that their past history and the past roles they had with each other no longer had meaning. It is playing "Let's Pretend" to suggest that who and what they have been to each other can be erased so that they are "free of all the personal junk" that is forever etched in their neurons and their feelings.

After our exploration of many facets of the relationship be-

* Barry Stevens, "Reflections on Unparenting," *Voices* 12(4): 69 (1976–1977).

tween parents and their adult children, her provocative words bring us back to the basic queries we asked at the beginning of this book: What's the parent of an adult for? And what are grown-up children for? In many species of the animal kingdom, once the parent has raised its young to the point where they can survive without him, there is no longer a special relationship; they go their separate and indifferent ways. And in terms of biology, once we have done our jobs of nurturing, rearing and launching our children so even if we were to die or they were to live on the other side of the world they could make it on their own, then no further involvement with them is necessary. And except for those situations where the children become our caretakers when we are aged or infirm, it is difficult to see what biological role they have in our lives.

But despite the lack of biological necessity, parents and their children usually remain deeply important to each other throughout the overlapping years of their life spans, and even beyond, because there is an incomparable history they share that is stored in conscious and unconscious memories. There are meanings they have for each other that arise from that history. And above all, there are profound feelings for each other that bridge gaps of time and distance, of conflict and change. Often there is a special kind of love. At times there is hate. And there may be disappointment, pride, guilt, respect, resentment—a myriad mixture of emotions that form the strands of that invisible cord which forever connects us. Rarely is there indifference. Rarely is there absence of feeling.

Entering the present moment between you and your child is all that "personal junk" from the past that Barry Stevens talks of, and often it is junk in the form of conceptions and misconceptions that grow out of past roles and keep you from truly seeing who your child is, and keep your child from really knowing who you are. But often that junk is gold, because it makes the relationship rich with nuances of empathic responsiveness, intuitions, compassion, understanding and commitment that is profoundly human, and has shaped the kind of persons we and our children are.*

* After reading the manuscript for this chapter, my friend Lori Jacobs sent me a note saying:

"When I looked back at a copy I have of Barry Stevens's article, I

The fact that there is a tie based on the past is not always positive. As we have seen earlier, hatred and anger and guilt can form a terribly strong bond which can destroy both parent and child. So if we are to learn what is the purpose of a relationship between a parent and an adult child, we must look not at those parents and offspring who have troubled relationships but at those whose relationships are mostly a source of joy and fulfillment for both. Whenever I interviewed parents who were happy about their relationships with their adult children, I sought clues as to what they did right. Certain themes emerged. None of these themes was true in all instances, but most of them were present whenever the parents expressed a basic pleasure in and contentment with their grown-up children.

He Is Separate

When I listened to these contented parents, perhaps the most consistent theme that came through was their ability to help their children become separate from them and then to appreciate their children's continued independent development. One mother, who has a satisfying relationship with her twenty-five-year-old daughter, said:

> She was born independent. When she was two years old she was doing things for herself. I love that. I love the independence of that particular child. I even admire the fact that she didn't want to sit down next to me and be read to. This is the child who learned to read earliest. She always had to be doing everything by herself. That kind of independence is something I thought was marvelous. She's twenty-five now. She doesn't live at home. When she finished college she went off.

Can you imagine how terrible the mother-daughter relationship would be if this young daughter, who had a lifelong striving for

---

saw that I had penciled in the margin 'but children who grow up and leave home need *both* freedom *and* roots.'

"This is brought forth so literally now in my house on the eve of Ilene's leaving for college. Her long-time interest in the genealogy of our family has, in the past few months (since college applications), been extremely intensified and accelerated."

independence, had a mother who needed to control her and keep her from being independent? They would have battled all the way, they would probably now be barely talking to each other, and the mother would be saying, "She was always stubborn and pigheaded. She acted like I was her enemy."

Now let's listen to this father who bowls with his son on the same team and who enjoys his relationship with him.

> I supervise a lot of people at work, and I have to fight my tendency to direct him—do it this way, do it that way. I mean sometimes, when he was a youngster, it was proper to tell him what to do because children need something different when they are two or twelve or twenty-two. But I knew it was important that I trust him to make his own decisions. Sometimes it was murder. He decided to quit college after one semester and bum around. That upset me but it was up to him. Then, after two years he said, "Folks, I need self-discipline and I can't give it to myself. I'm joining the army!" That really shook me up. It was a time everyone was trying to stay out. I told him he was wrong, wrong, wrong. But he knew it was his decision to make, not mine, and I knew it too. And now he's out of the army, and he has control of his life in a way that he never had before. He's got a good job, he's back in college nights, and he's got a nice girl friend he'll probably marry. He knew what was best for him, but that's besides the point. He might have chosen wrong. He might have gotten killed in the war or become a junkie over there. The thing is, it's his privilege to make those mistakes.

It's his privilege. His father recognized his son's birthright of independence.

Here is another father who also saw the importance of launching his three children.

> I'd say we kicked Andrew out of the house. Despite our affection for him, he was too dependent on us. And too much a "come home boy." This was his first year in graduate school and he lived home with us. It was convenient and cheap, but we felt it wasn't good for him, for somebody

> who was twenty-two to come home to elderly people and talk and watch TV and go to bed. . . . We almost had to throw Andy out of the house just because we felt the silk cord was too strong. While Marilyn you could not keep at home. When she got her first job, in a department store, she moved to Greenwich Village. And she loves it. It's such a swinging place, she continues to live there. That's for her. It would be a punishment for Marilyn to live home, although she's the most affectionate of the three. For Steve the issue hasn't come up yet, but I'm sure he wants to be independent at the earliest opportunity.

He Is Unique

Note that this father not only encourages and takes pleasure in his children's separateness from them—his parents—but he also sees them as separate and distinct from each other. He sees that Andrew, Marilyn and Steve are different people with different paces and needs in the separation process. This was another repeated theme among parents who were happy in their relationship with their adult sons and daughters. Rarely did you hear them refer to "the children" as a group. Each of their offspring was separate and unique, and they related to each of them accordingly.

I Trust Him

This kind of respect for the adult child as a separate, self-directed and special individual was perhaps put best by this mother of five grown-up progeny, all unusually successful people with a warm and easy relationship with her.

> I believe you have to trust your children. There's a kind of wisdom of the body or of the soul that can lead each person to what's best for him, particularly as he matures. Not that I kept my opinions out of it—I have very strong opinions. But they know that they can do it their way and that I'd never say, "I told you so."

As I listened to her, it was not difficult to understand why her children, all of whom now have children of their own, loved her and liked her so openly. They felt her trust in them, and so they deeply trusted her.

He Does Not Reflect on Me

In a parent group, one mother talked of how embarrassed she was that her son, at twenty-five, was still drifting around, usually high on drugs, and unable to find a direction for himself. She said, "It's not just concern—another thing is what the neighbors think. I'm being silly, but it's status, absolutely."

A second woman responded, "I never gave a damn about what people would think about me, based on what my kids did."

"Wouldn't you be embarrassed? Maybe you have more self-respect."

"I know I would not be embarrassed if say, Glen, who's about your boy's age, was still loafing around. I would really be upset in the sense of having the feeling, Where did I miss with him on a one-to-one basis? What went wrong all along the line—that this kid is still high on grass and roaming around all over the place, still doing nothing at age twenty-five? But I wouldn't give a hoot what the neighbors thought about what he was doing."

"I just say 'the neighbors' as a figure of speech," the first woman said. "I mean the people I care about. Like my parents and my sisters."

"I know what you mean. Maybe once I would have been upset about that, but I've changed. No longer do I feel my children can reflect glory on me, although I certainly do feel pride. But since I've given up the idea of their reflecting glory on me, neither can they make me feel ashamed or embarrassed. I feel they are who they are, and I love them, but I have to live with myself and what I do, not what they do."

It does not seem like a coincidence that the children of this second woman were more successful, effective people than those of the first woman, who had given her children the enormous burden of making her look good.

He Is Not an Extension of My Wishes

The parents with satisfying relationships with their children not only cared little about their sons or daughters reflecting glory on them, but neither did they see the children as extensions of their own wishes. Listen to these two fathers:

FATHER 1: "My whole family were academics. I am a professor of philosophy and value the intellectual life. But Ken got his degree in business administration and has entered the corporate world. It seems like a strange choice, but it's okay with me. He wasn't put here to live out my dreams, but to create his own."

FATHER 2: "Sure I hoped he'd go into my business and I was disappointed that he never showed much interest in it. Now he's about to get a doctorate in anthropology, and I know he'll make only one-fourth of what he could make in my business, but I can see he's happy with it. It's not what I would have done in his place, but he's not me."

Each father had almost the opposite script for his son, but each fully accepted his son's right to follow his own script. No wonder they both got along very well with their sons.

I Can Enjoy Who He Is

A mother of three children, ranging in age from eighteen to twenty-one said, "It's nice to sit back and see the life pattern they're beginning to form. They have a sense of humor and are great to talk to. It's very gratifying when they can come and kibbitz about their dates and they want us to know what's happening in their lives and they're comfortable. It's very nice." And her eyes sparkled with the enjoyment she had in who they were.

This sense of joy in who their children are came through again and again when parents reported that they had good relations with their children. Which came first, the children's being enjoyable or the parents' joy in them? It's probably a mixture of both, but there can be little doubt that parental enjoyment of who the child is can instill a sense of security in the child of any age and can evoke much love in that child toward the parent who finds such joy in his being.

Lack of Self-Centeredness

If we look at what has been said by these parents whose relationships with their grown-up offspring are going well, we see that they have repeatedly indicated that their children are separate, unique and enjoyable individuals, not put on earth to live out their parents' wishes or to make their parents look good. Evidently, reacting to their children in this way is the parents' contribution to the relationship's being a good one. What does it take for a parent to react in this salutary way?

It takes a certain kind of lack of self-centeredness on the part of the parent. I am not talking now about a healthy self-centeredness that arises out of liking and respecting oneself and trying to create a gratifying life. A lack of that type of self-centeredness leads to being a loser, a martyr, a frustrated and unfulfilled person. I am talking about the kind of self-centeredness that makes the parent see other people, particularly closely related people, as existing to satisfy his needs, wishes and expectations. I am talking about the kind of self-centeredness that obscures the boundaries between the parent and others so that he tends to assume that other people will see the world the same way he does, hold the same opinions and interests he does, enjoy what he enjoys, live the way he would have them live. In other words, this is the kind of self-centeredness that comes from the inner child of the parent, a remnant of that early childhood time when a person sees himself and his desires as the focal point of the universe and tries to control the world to meet those desires. When such inner child self-centeredness exists in a parent, I have usually found his relationship with his children to be a disaster area of anger and pain. Where there is a lack of this type of narcissism, when this type of egocentric inner child does not control the parent's behavior, I have usually found the relationship to be mutually loving, caring and respectful.

Here are the words of an eighty-year-old Chicago woman whose relationships with her children have been damaged by the persistent intrusion of her self-centered inner child. She is talking about a visit from her son, who had recently returned from a vacation in Europe.

> I can't make him out. I can't understand him. Of course, his ideas of life are different from mine. Like he and his wife have a season ticket for the ballet. And like when he came for lunch after he got back from his trip to Europe and he sat and talked and talked. He was telling me about France and Italy and how gorgeous and beautiful everything was, and the restaurants, and the Alps and all the beautiful things he's seen that he says he'll never forget for the rest of his life. He couldn't stop raving about it, but I stopped him to talk about visiting me more. His telling me about the beautiful scenery and showing me the pictures didn't interest me because I've never seen it, and what I didn't see I don't care about.

Is it any wonder that her son doesn't visit her more often? Her needy inner child's self-centeredness was so great that she could not allow herself to enter her son's frame of reference, to be stimulated by his enthusiasm, to learn something about who he is and what he enjoys, to expand her own horizons. It is not difficult to imagine that if she could have come out of her own constricted confines of self-involvement and had responded with excitement, curiosity, inquisitiveness, pleasure in his pleasure and happiness at his obvious enjoyment in sharing his experience with her, their relationship would be so much richer and deeper. That kind of parent would not have to push her children to see her. They simply would want to.

So, to a large degree, the absence of inner child self-centeredness may be seen as the key contribution a parent can make to a good relationship with his grown-up offspring.

I Can Count on Them

Time after time, what I would hear from parents who like their relationship with their children was a statement that when the chips were down, they could really count on their children to be there for them. Listen to this woman:

> My kids were so with me when my husband died. And he wasn't their father, you know. They were already grown when Donald and I were married, and it wasn't easy for them to let him into their lives at first, but they came to love him. . . . When Donald died they seemed everywhere. They were holding me, crying with me, calling people, making arrangements, everything. What was most important was the way they sat up with me into the night those first few awful days, letting me talk about him, and sharing their favorite stories about him. And they didn't just disappear. Though they had to get back to the other demands of their lives, they've been so with me, so sensitive to what I had lost.

What this mother is saying is that her adult children, in a time of crisis, came through for her in the same way they might for their dearest friend, and even more. This did not necessarily mean that they felt or acted as close friends in the ordinary contacts of day-to-day living before this disaster, but when there was tragedy, the bond created by their long-shared history, by the years of caring she had shown them, drew them to her automatically and nurturingly. And she could draw from the support and love of her children as perhaps she could from no one else. These children, at least in such circumstances, showed that lack of self-centeredness so vital to a close relationship. They were able to put aside the egocentric demands of their own inner children and respond to their mother with the mature parenting part of themselves.

He Can Count on Me

No matter how old our sons and daughters are, they would like to feel they can turn to us for support. And I am not referring only to the kind of support one adult may give another adult, be it emotional, practical, financial, or whatever. I am talking about a wish for support that arises out of the fact that we are his parents. I am referring to the fact that we have been in his life since day one, and we are deeply imprinted on his memory, deeply entrenched in his psyche. In other words, I am referring to his inner child who never dies and never disappears, and to whom we will always be the big parents whose love and approval he craves and whose disapproval he fears. Our children may be effective and mature adults; they may have long ago put aside any conscious awareness of these inner child needs; they may, in practical fact, need us for nothing. But the ineradicable inner child is still there, still responding to us as to no one else in this world.

Parents who have a good relationship with their offspring seem to know this and respond sensitively to it. This does not mean that they treat their grown-up sons and daughters like little children. They are respectful of them as adults, but know they have this special meaning for them. They know their earned praise is different from other people's praise, that their scorn pushes old buttons that can devastate the child within their child, that their understanding is peculiarly soothing and healing. And they are sensitive to those times when their child's inner child is in the foreground or is particularly needy.

A parent whose own inner child gets in the way cannot respond empathetically and helpfully to his son or daughter, and after a while his children will let these parents see very little of their neediness, their pain or their struggles. I couldn't keep count of the many times I have heard adults say, as did one woman of thirty-three, "My parents don't really want to know my troubles. My mother asks but she changes the subject if I tell her something she doesn't want to hear." This woman was hungry for sympathy and understanding from her mother, but her mother was unhearing and unresponsive because the mother's inner child did not want to be troubled, did not want the reality to be other than what she wished it to be, and did not want to be called on to be giving. By now this daughter has learned to feed her mother nothing but cheery and often untrue platitudes, which makes their relationship superficial and empty.

Another woman overheard her mother tell a friend, "I had two tragedies this year—my husband died and my daughter got a divorce." She was treating these events as if they were of the same magnitude! This daughter was not only overwhelmed by the realization of the gap between her mother's values and her own, but she knew that at a time when she, the daughter, ached to turn to her mother with her own hurt and worries, she could not because her mother was even more upset than she was. This mother's inner child had taken over, made her daughter's divorce a personal catastrophe of such proportions that she was not able to respond to her daughter with real support and backing at a time her daughter was most in need. "It felt awful," the daughter said. "I really needed a mother."

In the novel *Kinflicks,* Ginny's mother said she hoped Ginny had been well and happy.

> "I *have* been well and happy, Mother. In between being sick and miserable."
>
> "Oh well, that's life," she said glibly, closing the door on the topic.
>
> But wait! everything in me raged. *Why* don't you want to hear the ways in which I've been sick and miserable? Because I knew she didn't.*

So I cannot urge you strongly enough—and I don't care if your children are in their teens or their fifties—to recognize this unique and special role you have in their psyches and souls. You have been etched early in the memory cells of your children, when those cells were fresh and almost blank, and when you were their whole world. Now they may be parents or grandparents themselves, they may be important people and they may have accom-

* Lisa Alther, *Kinflicks,* p. 401.

plished great things; perhaps you hardly see them, perhaps there has been conflict and estrangement. But you still have this special meaning to that forever little child who dwells within them, and your respectful, nonpatronizing responsiveness to this dimension of the relationship can bring the two of you much closer.

He Appreciates My Wisdom

I was sitting with a group of people I know well, who ranged in age from their mid-twenties to their early fifties. The conversation had developed into one in which they were complaining about their parents, mostly humorously, often with a kind of laughing exasperation. At one point I said, "You're all talking about what a pain in the neck your parents can be and how they can drive you up the wall. And not one of you is financially dependent on them. You all have busy, full lives without them. So what do you need them for?"

The conversation turned serious and many answers were given to my question, but among those who felt they had a particularly good relationship with their parents, one of the consistent responses was similar to that of this woman, a forty-five-year-old mother of three:

> Very often, I find she has a lot to say about some of the problems I run into in my life. I mean personal problems. Sometimes they're very practical problems, but usually there's some conflict in me about it. And so I call her long distance. . . . My mother may not be the most brilliant person in the world, but she always has a way of looking at it, a clear perspective that I find helpful. I think it's simply that she's lived longer and been through a lot of it.

This woman's husband, who was also participating in the conversation, said, "And she cares about you so she wants to give you the best advice. And she knows you very, very well. I find it the same with my parents. I am more successful in business than my father ever was, but I've usually talked to him before making changes and he almost always zeros in on the main issue and gives me good advice." He turned to his wife—about whom everyone there knew he cared very much and said, "Except about you. When he met you that first time, he told me, 'That young woman has quality.' But he can't be right all the time."

The group laughed and several others gave instances of valuing their parents' judgment. I noted that these were the people with the easiest, more satisfying relationships with their parents. And then I thought of a couple I had interviewed because I had been told they had an enviably good relationship with their five grown children. As part of their answer to my question as to what the children still needed them for, the father said, "I'm going to use an old-fashioned word. Wisdom. That may sound arrogant, but I have lived twenty-five years longer than the oldest of them, forty years longer than the youngest of them, and I've accumulated a lot of knowledge. No. Knowledge isn't it. All five of them are professionals and have more knowledge than me. It's wisdom. I guess that's knowledge plus experience plus a way of looking at things. At any rate, they often turn to us for it and expect it to be there and often it is. Sometimes they want to see it there when we don't have it and sometimes I can't discourage them from thinking so, but I always tell them when I feel my view doesn't feel solid. That's wisdom too."

You have lived longer than your children, and you care about what happens to them. They would want the benefit of your accumulated wisdom if they have not been so caught up in a Song or Dance with you that they automatically reject anything you have to say, or if your inner child has so often dominated your more mature judgment that your son or daughter does not respect your views. But your children would like to find this wisdom in you, and if your mature perspective can preside, you can have something to offer of great value, as in the stories of times long ago, when the elders passed the fruits of their sagacity to the next generation.

We Can Have Fun Together

A father of four said, "There's a great deal of laughter in my house. We are cards. And it's sort of fun to be there. When the boys brought girls or the girls brought their boys, they had that feeling, too. The Seaver house is a nice place for young people to be, and I think it just survived even though three of them are out now."

Where parents talked of a history of having fun with their children, they almost always had good relationships with their children as adults. And they are still having fun. Because besides being able to be there for each other in crises, beyond the mutual respect and in addition to your offering your wisdom, it adds so much warmth to a relationship if you can play and laugh together. In *Something Happened,* Joseph Heller's hero is musing to himself about his relationship with his son.

> . . . I have noted that people grew up much the way they begin; and hidden somewhere inside every bluff or quiet man and woman I know, I think, is the fully formed, but uncompleted, little boy or girl that once was and will always remain as it always has been, suspended lonesomely inside its own past, waiting hopefully, vainly, to resume, longing insatiably for company, pining desolately for that time to come when it will be safe and sane and possible to burst out exuberantly, stretch its arms, fill its lungs with invigorating air, without fear at last, and call:
>
> "Hey! Here I am. Couldn't you find me? Can't we be together now?"
>
> And hiding inside of me somewhere, I know (I feel him inside me. I feel it beyond all doubt), is a timid little boy just like my son who wants to be his best friend and wishes he could come outside and play.*

So in this area, the inner child doesn't interfere with the relationship but adds immeasurably to it. Because in us is a joyful, playful child who can come out, find the joyful, fun-loving child inside our grown-up son or daughter, and laugh together till our eyes sparkle and our cheeks glow.

* Joseph Heller, *Something Happened* (New York: Ballantine, 1975), p. 213.

We Can Disagree

Parents who speak contentedly of their relationships with their children do not paint these relationships as all warm and toasty, all full of laughs and conflict-free. There are frequently disagreements. But what I do hear from them are such phrases as:

> "Sometimes he makes me furious but in our family we just don't hold grudges."
>
> "We can disagree but that's okay. After all, we're different people."
>
> "We don't always see eye to eye but we never lose sight of the big picture—which is that we love each other."

This ability to accept the conflicts and clashes with their children as an inevitable part of any good relationship rather than to see it as an outrage, a tragedy, a betrayal, a disaster, a cause for chronic pain or a reason for provoking guilt often differentiated parents with good relationships with their grown-up children from those with disappointing relationships.

And closely akin to being able to disagree is the ability to forgive and to allow ourselves to be forgiven. Listen to the words of this middle-aged woman.

> I have a fantasy, a lifelong fantasy, that someday my mother or my father will say to me, in these exact words, "I forgive you, I forgive you for everything you ever did, you are totally forgiven and I still love you." A year after my husband's death, I was in Atlanta to be with my mother and I don't think that was coincidental. I probably went there to get a little mothering or something, and my mother and I were sort of kidding around and laughing. And my mother, who was a very undemonstrative woman, walked toward me and said, "Peggy, I love you. Will you forgive me for everything I did wrong?" Now I don't know, was *I* forgiven? I still don't know. My fantasy is unfulfilled. It was a beautiful moment, but I don't know where I stand.

Certainly it seems that Peggy was forgiven. But she needed the words concretely. Maybe love means never having to say you're sorry, but it often is a loving thing to *want* to say. And particularly in a parent-child relationship, even the best of them, there are so many times when each has hurt the other and both carry wounds and both carry guilt. Perhaps the relationship is close enough so that the forgiveness is understood and need not be put into words. But spoken or unspoken, in a fulfilling relationship, it is always there.

We Love Each Other

When the relationship between a parent and his grown-up child is good, what all these discrete components we've been looking at add up to is the same as what they would add up to in any good relationship—love. Not soupy, sentimental love, although sometimes such feelings may be present. But if you feel that you have a loving relationship with your child, you know it as a deep concern with the well-being and fulfillment of that child, not for who he is to you but who he is in himself. This means seeing him not as a person who must gratify your needs, but as someone who must become more successful at achieving his own self-realization. So whether we are talking of your love for your child or your child's love for you, we do not find, in listening to those parents who are pleased about their relationship with their child, much evidence of the inner child's dependent, controlling love, but indications of a mature, freestanding love.

In this mature love, the recognition that we are each separate and autonomous is paramount, but this does not mean uninvolvement. This love is the deepest kind of involvement and caring. I remember the eminent psychologist Carl Rogers, reflecting on his seventieth birthday about what he has learned and where he is trying to go. He spoke eloquently of being able increasingly to allow people to be themselves, with no attempt to control them, and in so doing finding more and more beauty in them. He talked of the almost universal pleasure people find in sunsets and how so much of that pleasure is because we don't control the sunset: It happens, it unfolds. He noted that we would lose so much of that pleasure if we could add a dab of some color or take away a little of another color. So it is with us and our children, no matter what their age or ours. In our mature parental love we enjoy, but do not need to control, their unique unfolding. In this kind of love, we are all miracles, and we can see and be astonished at the miracle of our child.

But such mature love is *not* selfless. We can want for ourselves, too. In fact, we must want for ourselves, or we will soon be serving our children, denying our own needs, forfeiting the actualization of our own souls and the fulfillment of our personal goals. Nor does maturely loving our children mean we must accept mistreatment from them or surrender to any exploitation. Such martyrdom can bring about the death of love.

And mature parental love is not blind. It entails seeing your child whole. You will know him all too well, though never well enough. You may see much that you do not like, even that you may abhor. And if there is too much that you find offensive, your love may erode like once-rich topsoil starved to dust, for you are not obliged to love him no matter what. He may not be very lovable. But if you have stopped loving him because your inner child needed him to be a certain way and has been disappointed, then if you can transcend that sad or sulking child within you and accept your offspring for who he is, you may be able—at times passively, at times actively—to delight in the existence of your son or daughter in the world and in your life.

We Go Beyond Ourselves

One last time let us ask, What is the parent of an adult for? And what is an adult child for?

The relationship with our child gives us the ongoing opportunity, from the day he is born to the present moment and tomorrow's moments, to grow beyond the limits of the child within us who sees others only as need satisfiers, to stretch our horizons wider than our tiny self-interest and to encompass another human with as much caring as for ourselves. Our relationship with our child is not the only relationship that can help us grow in this way, but it can foster that growth like no other if we let it.

And we can have the gratification of knowing the special and indelible place we have in the thoughts and memories and feelings of our sons or daughters no matter their age.

And we can look out on the bigger space we have in the world because of our children, and we can see the rainbow of our continuity arcing into the future through them.

And if the relationship is good, we and they have a friend like no one else.

CHAPTER 11

Going My Way

A woman I know had just put her youngest child, a boy of eleven, on the bus that was to take him to camp for the summer, and she stood outside the bus weeping, already missing him. Her son slid the bus window open and said to her, "Look mother, you can have a very good summer—if you want to!"

The words of this sophisticated eleven-year-old boy can serve as a keynote for all parents whose children are departing or have departed from the close, dependent, deeply involved relationship of an earlier time. In his wisdom he is telling you and me that we have a choice: We can either weep and bemoan the loss of the old closeness and thus attempt to cling to it, or we can use the newly acquired freedom to go out and create another fulfilling phase of life—if we want to.

Many sages tell us of the importance of letting go and being separate from our children. In the *New Testament* Jesus says, "He that loveth father or mother more than me is not worthy of me; and he that loveth son or daughter more than me is not worthy of me."* Jesus is not preaching intrafamilial discord or

* Matthew, 10:57

indifference. He is recognizing the fact of each person's separateness and the sacred right of every individual to set aside even the closest of emotional ties if those ties keep him from pursuing his own way, his own life and his own truth. And by implication, is he not saying that we each have the duty to loosen those ties when they fetter another from this pursuit?

Kahlil Gibran tells us:

Your children are not your children.
They are the sons and daughters of Life's longing for itself.
They come through you but not from you,
And though they are with you they belong not to you.*

And the eleven-year-old boy was telling us that we can choose to find joy, renewal and fulfillment in our separateness. We listen to these sages of ancient and recent days, of mature years and of few years, and we agree with their message that we and our children are individuals, each with his own path to follow, but even though we agree, something in us balks, some part of us feels sad and frightened as we watch our children develop lives and interests and relationships that take them further away from us.

Our reaction is understandable on many levels. We can feel the nostalgia for the days when our child had the special cuteness and freshness of being small and when we were so indisputably and unwaveringly the center of his universe. In the changes in him even more strikingly than in the changes in ourselves, we can see time passing. We can be sad at the real loss of day-to-day closeness with someone with whom we shared so much for so long. And finally, our inner child, who fears abandonment and who desperately wants to cling to those he has been dependent on for nurturance, that little child in us will cry out at the departure of the grown child out there. And if our inner child takes over, we may be tempted to continue or revive those old Songs and Dances and begin to provoke guilt or fear or shame in order to restore our control and maintain the tie.

But we have seen that Songs and Dances, even when they

* Kahlil Gibran, *The Prophet* (New York: Knopf, 1923), p. 17.

work to keep our children intensely involved with us, carry a high emotional price tag. The cost may be in all kinds of bad feelings on both sides—anger, hate, defiance, hurt, bitterness, disappointment—bad feelings that kill the old dream that there would always be a loving closeness between ourselves and our child. But still, if we give up on trying to maneuver or command this closeness, then what do we have? We have lost something precious, but have we gained anything worth having?

The answer is yes, we have gained a great deal. Those words about gaining greater freedom to discover and develop ourselves and to create a new life that is appropriate to the age and stage we are now at are not empty words. If you would refute them by pointing to all those who, their children gone and not particularly close, are leading sad and lonely lives, I would have to agree that there are many, many people like that. For recognizing the separateness of ourselves and our children is no guarantee that we will have a new fulfillment; it only gives us the option. Countless parents never choose that option. Countless parents for so many years have depended on their fulfillment through the role of mother or father, or the closeness or achievements of their children that they don't even recognize they have other options. So they experience only the sad part of it, the loss, the death of something, and not the opportunity for a rebirth. That is tragic and a waste.

The alternatives that open up when parents recognize the freedom they have gained from standing separately are in two areas: the new possibilities *outside of* their relationship with their children and the new possibilities *in* their relationship with their children.

New Options Outside of the Children

When we stop thinking of gaining our fulfillment largely through our relationship with our children, we face ourselves with powerful questions that we may not have asked for a long time, questions like: What do I want? What makes me happy? What makes me unhappy? Am I satisfied with my life? How would I like to change it? Do I dare?

The issues will be more specific, depending on who we are and where we are. If you are married, you and your spouse may have to really face each other without the buffer of your concern for and involvement with your children, without assuming the practiced role of mother and father. Perhaps you have been using your children and your parenthood to avoid that for many years. It can be a time of rediscovery, of creating anew a relationship based on standing together as man and woman instead of as father and mother.

There is the possibility that what you find in this rediscovery you will not like. You may find that you immersed yourself so deeply in your parental role to keep from noticing that you could not stand your spouse, that he doesn't love you, that there is an unbridgeable emptiness between you. New options carry no guarantees of rose gardens, no promises of permanence. They might face you with new decisions, like whether you should stay together or separate, because the societal changes that have made the possibility of divorce so much more acceptable in your children's generation have now made it more acceptable in yours.

I have seen instances where parents begin to seek their primary fulfillment apart from their children, and their marriage gets closer, deeper, more obviously enjoyable as they are each free to be fully and pleasurably with each other; and I have seen instances where, after the children's autonomy has been accepted, the parents find little to hold them together. Fortunately, I have seen more of the first, but either way, the people involved are facing their lives honestly, accepting their lives as they are now instead of holding on to the past bonds with their children for their security or sense of purpose. Either way, they are taking the risk of finding their identity other than in being a parent.

Married or single, the questions of what do we really want and how would we like to change things can enter every aspect of our lives.

- Do we have the friendships we like? Would we like new ones? Different kinds of friendships? How do we get them?

- Do we like how we spend our time? If we don't work, would we like to? If we do work, would we like not to? Do we want to change our work now that the responsibility for our children is not a consideration?

- Do we like the degree of freedom and mobility we have? Do we want more?

- Do we participate in recreation, hobbies, or social activities that we find enjoyable and satisfying? Why not? How can we change that? Is there something we've always wanted to learn more about, or how to do? How can we go about that?

The possibilities are great and exciting when we realize that our children's freedom to be separate is a gift of freedom to us. Freedom is almost always scary. It presents the possibility of leaving the safe and familiar for the untried and unknown. That involves risks. We can succeed or fail. We can feel effective or inadequate. We might have to face our terror of aloneness. In *Cutting Loose* I wrote about accepting our separateness from our parents, but the same words would apply to us as parents accepting the separateness of our children:

> . . . That ending and that new beginning face you with what Kierkegaard called "the alarming possibility of being able." And why is being able alarming? Because it means breaking with all the messages you grew up with that say, "Don't," "You can't," "You're too little." You may have been rooted in muck all this time but it has been familiar muck. Who you were, what was expected of you, and what limitations you had to accept were all too clearly marked. Breaking with all this means facing the unknown and, by yourself, without the aid of your old and timeless fixed stars, using only your own feelings and judgment, daring to navigate through terrifying, uncharted and unpredictable space. Being able means severing the vestigial ties that leash you to the past, and standing upright, knowing your ultimate aloneness, knowing your weaknesses and your strengths, daring to turn your wishes and your potentials toward untried risks. If that isn't alarming, what is? *

* Howard Halpern, *Cutting Loose*, p. 254.

Very alarming. But that freedom beckons, and we can choose to exercise as few or as many new options as we wish. Some parents have made major changes. For example, listen to this mother of three children, the youngest twenty-two.

> They're all out now, and two live far away. . . . At first I was angry at them for not having much room for me in their lives, and one day when I was up on the second floor looking at their rooms, actually looking at their empty rooms and feeling sorry for myself like in a soap opera scene, I realized I was keeping their rooms like shrines—and that was crazy. If they had their lives, then I could have mine. I began to think of what I want now, in the next chapter. . . . I'm so fortunate. At a time in my life when I thought everything would be going downhill, I'm involved with my work and studies. I love going to school. I could go to school forever. I'm still involved, less now than I used to be, in my husband's business. I lead a busy, busy life. As I said, I feel very fortunate.

Sometimes the new options are not as major, but just as renewing and exciting. Listen to this mother of two adult sons.

> I've found things in myself that I'd never allowed to come out, ways in which I could have been happier, more productive—productive is not the word—had more pleasures than I had allowed myself. For example, I never did anything athletic because I thought of myself as clumsy and now—at first out of just a need to be busy—I play tennis. Too bad I didn't do that before. It's a hell of a lot of fun. And the same with other things.

And a father of four grown children said:

> I'm in a profession where I can make my own schedule. Now that the last child is out, I don't feel we have to be around during the school week. I get all my work done in three-and-a-half days or less, and we take these long weekends up at the cabin, from Thursday afternoon or night till Monday afternoon, sometimes even till Tuesday morning. It's nice, just the two of us. At times, one or more of the

> kids will come up for Saturday or Sunday but mostly we're alone. . . . Besides enjoying the lake or woods, I do the writing I always dreamed of. I just had one small piece published and now I just got an advance for a book. I've shifted into another gear and I love it.

That's what this newly opened option is all about—the opportunity to shift into another gear, one based on your needs, your wishes, your circumstances, your bents; one made of old dreams, long buried beneath the rituals, demands and habits of parenthood. And if you get in touch with this part of yourself and follow it, you, too, may love it.

A New Beginning with Your Children

The cultural fluidity that has allowed our children to break with many past prescriptions for what their relationship with us should be liberates us, as well, from these prescriptions and presents us with the possibility of looking freshly at our children and considering how we would like the relationship to be. For example, we have seen that our children are relieved of some of the societal restraints that enjoined earlier generations to remain closely and respectfully devoted to their parents no matter what; instead they will maintain the kind of relationship with us that emerges from their own feelings about us and who we are as people. By the same token, we are freed to maintain the kind of relationship that grows out of our feelings about them and who they are as people. While the unique past history of who we have been to them and who they have been to us can never be overlooked (nor should it be) and while some cultural guidelines will always influence the relationship, there is now considerable latitude. And while our children may feel freer, and suffer little societal condemnation if they limit contact with us because they don't like how we are with them, we also are freer and would suffer less societal condemnation than would have been true a few decades ago, should we limit contact with them if we don't like how they are being with us.

Put that way, it sounds negative. But let's turn it over and look at the other side of this newly minted cultural coin. Since we can't dictate the terms of the relationship, cannot command them to be "good children" according to our definition, and cannot coerce their love, and since they cannot dictate the terms of the relationship to us, cannot command us to be "good parents" according to their definition, and cannot coerce our love, we must, if we are to have any relationship at all, really learn to see each other, to know each other, and to talk to each other as adult individuals. We are challenged to look and listen and dare to expose our inner thoughts and feelings the way we would in any other relationship we wished was close and open. We are invited to be authentically ourselves with our children, and we can invite them to be authentically themselves with us. A thirty-nine-year-old woman told me of a conversation with her father in which she complained about the emptiness of the relationship and that he never really talks to her.

FATHER: I don't talk to you but you don't talk to me.

DAUGHTER: I stopped telling you about me because you always give me advice. I want your support, not your advice. I want you to listen and try to know who I am.

FATHER: But when I try to tell you about some of the things that are worrying me, you don't want to hear it either. You just tell me I shouldn't think that way.

DAUGHTER: Is that true? Then maybe it's time for us both to listen and not stop the other from talking. Let's try to get to really know each other.

We stand challenged to have a relationship based not on rules and roles, but on our being fully and openly there with our child, to invite our child to be fully and openly there with us, to look at our child clearly, and to discover how we feel about him and how he is as a person.

A Loving Separateness

It is not only the dissolution of the old societal guiding principles that now beckons us with the possibilities of a new kind of relationship with our children. These fresh possibilities are also created whenever we end an outworn and frustrating Song and Dance. By definition, a Song and Dance is between the child within us and the child within our son or daughter. So by definition it is kid stuff, limited in its range, its depth, its honesty and its maturity. Perhaps our inner child has been trying to control the relationship by commanding or belittling or blaming or shaming. Perhaps the inner child in our son or daughter has been defiant or demanding or distancing or dependent. Whatever the Song and Dance that has developed from these inner child needs, it prevents the adult us from interacting with the adult him or her. We know that it is difficult to set aside those Songs and Dances, and it feels hazardous to enter a new realm of relating. But exhilarating things can happen when we move to liberate ourselves from those outworn and deadly rituals.

One woman, speaking of her adult daughter, said, "I got tired of pushing and coercing—Come to see me, Call me, Where were you? Who are you going out with? and other things I felt driven to say. I always felt I was pushing where I wasn't wanted, and then suddenly one day I felt, I don't want to be where I'm not wanted. And I wasn't needed, either. My daughter had made her Declaration of Independence loud and clear and just like that—after I went for I don't know how long trying to hold on to the past—I realized that her Declaration of Independence was my Declaration of Independence. I could feel the relief that I no longer had the responsibility of 'raising her' or looking after her. I was free *not* to be a mother or act like a mother and I could just be me. I'm not sure how it worked, but we've gotten along so beautifully since then."

Yes, our children's Declaration of Independence liberates us if we dare to let it. That doesn't inevitably lead to a more satisfying relationship; sometimes it leads to greater distance if each finds little to hold him there. But children need both their autonomy *and* a connection with us, though often they can only affirm that need for a connection when they feel sure they have achieved their autonomy. And we also need our autonomy and our connection with them, but often we can only achieve a true, honest, unforced connection when we have accepted their freedom and embraced our own. That kind of freedom with that kind of connection makes for an invisible but strong tie between ourselves and our adult sons and daughters. We are attached by caring, not strings. We stand in a loving relationship at enough distance so that each can see the other clearly in the spankingly crisp space between us and around us, yet close enough to reach out and touch each other with our fingertips or our eyes, close enough to offer a hand in support when it is needed, close enough so that with a single step, we can embrace each other when our feelings call us to it. A loving separateness. It is what a relationship between us and our grown-up children can be.

About the Author

Howard M. Halpern received his Ph.D. in clinical psychology from Columbia University in 1954 and has been on the staff of several hospitals and clinics, as well as on the faculties of Columbia University, Finch College, and the Metropolitan Institute for Psychoanalytic Studies. From 1962 to 1977 he was the co-director of the New York Student Consultation for Psychotherapy and is now their consultant in parent-child relationships. He is a former president of the American Academy of Psychotherapists and has had many writings in psychotherapy and related topics published, both as articles and in books. His widely read book, *Cutting Loose: An Adult Guide to Coming to Terms with Your Parents,* was published in 1977.

A native New Yorker, Dr. Halpern has practiced psychotherapy in New York City for the past twenty-five years.